A Guide to Life

African Proverbs Made Relevant Today

Mind, Body & Spirit
Kesi Steven

A Guide to Life: African Proverbs Made Relevant Today

Copyright © 2021: Kesi Steven

First Printed in United Kingdom 2021

Published by Conscious Dreams Publishing
www.consciousdreamspublishing.com

Edited by Elise Abram
Typeset by Amit Dey

ISBN: 978-1-913674-55-7 (Paperback)
ISBN: 978-1-913674-56-4 (E-book)

Dedication

I dedicate this book to my sister, Nadine Steven; although we never had the opportunity to meet here on earth, I know you have been guiding me throughout my life from the spiritual plane. Thank you for your continued love, support, and protection.

—Ase

Table of Contents

Acknowledgements

————◆◆◆————

A special thanks to my dad; without your help, none of this would have been possible.

This idea came about in February 2020. My father and I were sitting in a restaurant, discussing what I wanted to write whilst waiting for our meal.

I gave my dad three different ideas of what I wanted to do, and I was struggling to pick just one. He simply said, 'Why don't you put all of these ideas into one, then?'

So, that is what I did. I put African proverbs, words of advice and affirmation, into one blog concept and started writing. A simple conversation turned into something amazing that I never knew was possible. The words came out like water as if I were destined to write this. I was shocked and mad at myself because I realised I had been sitting on this gift all my life without using it.

My dad was also my first proofreader and editor. Although he had his own work to do, he always found the time to read every lesson, checking for spelling mistakes, helping to ensure that what I wrote made sense.

My dad has always been my biggest supporter, always providing me with the space and freedom to find my own path, and I am grateful for it.

A special thanks to Emmanuel for providing a creative space for me to truly express myself. All that you said was, 'You can write whatever you want to write, and I'll post it.' That, alone, was enough to bring about this whole idea of turning African proverbs into modern-day lessons. What was originally a weekly blog post online turned into a whole book in less than a year. It is funny how life turns out, and it is true that all it takes is one person to make a difference in your life.

Lastly, I would like to thank all of my family, friends, teachers, colleagues, and those of you who I do not know for reading my original blogs. Your support and feedback are the main reason I chose to turn these lessons into a book. I wanted you to have something solid that you could hold and always refer back to when you need to. I pray that you have all learned something from these lessons. I, myself, learnt so much from writing them down, and I continue to push myself to practice what I preach.

Let this book be a reminder that anything is possible when you first believe in yourself, a reminder that God has provided you with all you need to be successful in life. All you have to do is listen to and follow your intuition.

A reminder that life is not one straight journey—there will be many twists, turns, and bumps—but you must embrace those moments as this is what makes you into the person you are destined to be.

Preface

--------◆◦◆--------

The key to the journey of life is to seek the knowledge of those who have experienced life before us. Our elders have passed down many wise words and teachings throughout time and history. The time has come for us to listen intently, rather than try to figure things out on our own.

Know that the words of our elders can best prepare us for the many challenges we may face throughout our life's journeys.

One form of teaching is African proverbs, which are deeply rooted in African history. These small but powerful gems of wisdom have been passed down from generation to generation and have been used to share ideas, give advice, inspire, and support those who have received them.

In essence, our elders have provided us with a guide to life, a handbook full of tips on how to handle the situations and challenges we may face, including family, relationships, peace, love, life, careers, society, and self. The beautiful thing about African proverbs is that they are open to interpretation and can have multiple meanings. Within this book, I have written one interpretation for each proverb and have given a modern-day breakdown. You can apply these lessons to your everyday life and pass them on to those who may need a few words of wisdom to guide them.

So, whether you are reading this book in 2021, 2030, or 2540, these lessons will always be relevant, and they will help guide you on your life's journey.

> 'A proverb is the horse that can carry one swiftly to the discovery of ideas.'
>
> —Nigerian proverb

Lesson 1

'When the shepherd comes home in peace, the milk is sweet.'

—**Ethiopian proverb**

*P*eace of mind doesn't come easily in this world. There are many factors that cause one to stress, worry, and doubt one's capabilities.

Work, family, relationships, school, friends, and the environment itself can all affect us negatively. Many of us allow these stressors to take over our minds and lives, but it is important to note that stress is always dependent upon your attitude towards the problem at hand. This means that you do not have to let these things or people affect your peace of mind. You can simply prevent the negative feelings from taking over by adjusting how you think about that person, thing, or situation.

Peace of mind is defined as 'being in a mental state of calmness or tranquility, and freedom from worry' ("Peace of Mind" 2020).

Take a moment to think about what peace of mind looks like to you. Think about the areas in your life that are not at peace and what needs to be done to create and/or restore peace in your life. It is also important to take a moment to reflect on how your stress and negative energy can affect those around you and disrupt their peace of mind.

When we have peace of mind, it simply means that we have the right balance within ourselves, and we have created an environment within ourselves through which only positive energy is allowed to shine.

Only then can everything flow naturally, our ideas, goals, and prayers can be achieved, and the journey of the shepherd can be one of peace.

Affirmation: I will not allow anything to affect my peace of mind.

Lesson 2

———◆———

'When there is no enemy within, the enemies outside cannot hurt you.'

—African proverb

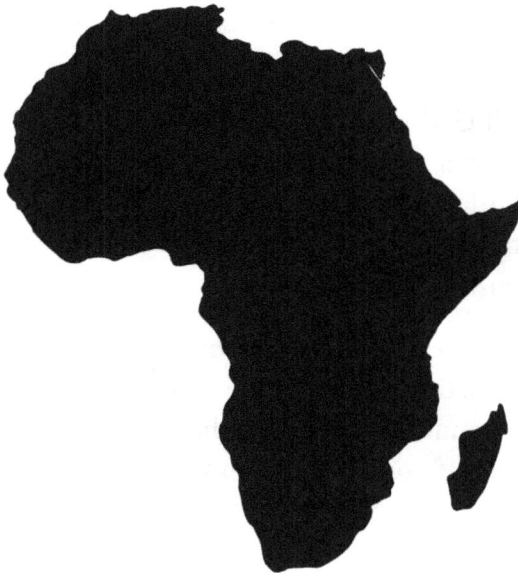

S imply put, you are your own worst enemy. This is a statement that carries a lot of weight and truth, but rather than look within some choose to place the blame on 'the outsiders', 'the haters', those who oppose our ideas. You must understand that fear, doubt, and worry are your true and worst enemies. You will not find them on the outside, and you will never see them in person, because they live within your mind, and they will challenge you every day.

Fear of the unknown, doubting yourself and your abilities, worrying about what other people might think or what could go wrong blocks you from reaching your goals and being successful in life. Take a moment to think of all the times you blocked a blessing by allowing doubt, fear, and worry to enter your mind. Think of all the times an opportunity was presented to you—maybe it was a new job, a new relationship, a chance to travel or explore and the like—and your immediate reaction was to question, doubt, and find fault rather than embrace and welcome something new. Don't worry because it happens to the best of us but know that there is work to be done.

To remove this enemy from within, you must first understand three things:

Firstly, we are all God's children. God protects us and guides us and will never give you a task or opportunity you can't handle. If there is a time when you feel lost, scared, anxious, or if you are struggling, speak to God and ask for assistance as God is always willing and able to help you when you need it.

Secondly, rather than fear the unknown, simply open your mind and heart to it. Embrace the unknown with your whole being. Stare it dead in the eye and step into it because as the saying goes, you will never know until you try. If you always stop yourself from trying, then you will never know, and you will miss out on countless experiences.

Lastly, when these fears, doubts, and worries enter your mind, identify what the issue is, pause your thoughts, and say out loud, 'I will not allow these negative thoughts to take over,' and 'I embrace all opportunities that come my way with an open mind.'

It is a natural part of human nature to be afraid, but you mustn't allow that fear to stop you from experiencing life. Once you learn how to remove the enemy from within, you create space for love, self-confidence, peace of mind, and positive thought to manifest, and that is more than enough to discourage enemies on the outside from attacking and disrupting your life's journey.

Affirmation: I will keep my mind open to all opportunities life has to offer.

Lesson 3

—◆—

'However long the night may last, there will be a morning.'

—African proverb

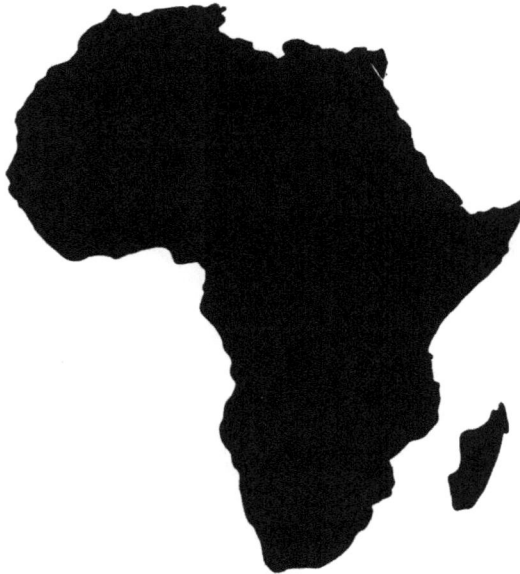

At this moment in time, the world is at a complete standstill as the earth is in the midst of a global pandemic. Many people have been grievously ill, and many have unfortunately died because of this virus. Businesses have been forced to shut down, health care systems are under pressure, schools are closed, and many countries have been shut off and placed into lockdown.

This pandemic has forced the world to be in a state of stillness mixed with fear and extreme vulnerability as you unwillingly place your life and welfare in the hands of the government and world leaders. This is similar to being in a nightmare that you cannot control, or from which you cannot escape, and it seems like it will never end.

Welcome to the long night—are you afraid?

It is within human nature to fear the night. It is a part of our DNA, buried deep within our psyches. 'In the past it was a vital survival trait needed to protect oneself from predators who dwell at night' (Hrla 2016); however, this is not the case now. Though we are on top of the food chain, the fear still lives within us, but it has manifested into something no longer physical but more psychological. It is the fear of the unknown, being blind to our surroundings, left alone with nothing but our minds that have the tendency to play tricks on us, and during this pandemic, the fear of illness, death, debt, and people.

My message to you is not to be afraid of this long night. Do not fear this moment of uncertainty. Do not fear what you cannot control. Do not dwell in the darkness of your mind and fear. Seek the light at the end of this tunnel, no matter how long the walk may be. The world is going through a struggle right now, and the only way to overcome a struggle is to change the narrative, think positively, and embrace this time of stillness.

Understand that you have been provided with a break, an opportunity, a chance to reflect on your life's journey, a moment to spend some quality time with yourself, time to work on and improve your health, and most importantly, a moment to breathe. How you use this time is up to you: set some goals, educate yourself, build stronger connections with your family, practice patience and self-love, or simply relax. Take each day as it comes and find peace where you can.

All I ask is that you have faith that this will all soon be over. Know that you will leave this nightmare as the best version of yourself, ready to tackle anything that comes your way.

Just as the virus came, it, too, shall pass, the world will move and keep on turning as if nothing happened. Understand that where there is night, there will always be day, where there is darkness, there is always light, and it is up to you to decide where you wish to dwell.

Affirmation: No matter how dark the night, I will always look for the light at the end of the tunnel.

Lesson 4

—◆—

'Having a good discussion is like having riches.'

—African proverb

*T*he truth is that conversations are not simply talking and listening. They are more of an art form, a skill that needs to be taught, learnt, and developed. Some people have a natural talent for it and can discuss anything with anyone without hesitation or fear. Others find it hard to have good, lasting, enriching conversations. Having a good discussion is rare in comparison to the amount of daily pointless conversations you have in which you forget half the things that were said, the topic of conversation did not engage you, or you did not want to talk to the person in the first place.

A good discussion should feel like your mind is being fed countless amounts of delicious food you have never had before, each morsel tasting better than the last. No matter the topic of discussion, you should feel so drawn into what the person has to say that the world around you is completely silent, and you can focus your full attention on the conversation at hand whilst preparing to provide your own ideas, critiques, and words of wisdom, as conversations are, of course, a two-way thing.

It is time to reflect on the people with whom you have surrounded yourself in the past, as well as those with whom you surround yourself in the present, be they family, friends, acquaintances, or coworkers. Whether they are in your life for a brief minute, months, years, or a lifetime, they can all affect your development and the way you think, simply by the types of conversations in which you engage. Think about the conversations you have had with these people from day to day. Think about how many times you were left feeling like your mind had been fed that delicious new food or the times you were completely drawn into the conversation and left feeling satisfied.

It is impossible to have a one-sided discussion, meaning that we all have a part to play to have a good, enriching conversation. It is time to reflect on the role you played in those conversations, and if you were able to reciprocate what you experienced. Did you provide your own insight? Did you ask questions? Did you feed your own batch of delicious food? Did you enrich someone else's mind? Were you able to leave the other person feeling equally satisfied with the conversation?

Having a good discussion that leaves a lasting memory and deeply engages is not easy to experience on a daily basis, but once you have truly had these types of enriching conversations, you will not want to go back to ordinary noise or chit-chat. It is important to treat communication as a skill to be learnt and constantly developed. It is equally important to surround yourself with people who can reciprocate or provide more sustenance in the discussions in which you engage.

Take the time you now have to make these necessary changes to improve the life you are currently living. Remove and avoid the people who do not enhance your mind and push yourself to seek those who do, as they will provide all the riches your mind seeks.

Affirmation: I surround myself with people who uplift and help me to become the best version of myself.

Lesson 5

—•◦•—

'If the full moon loves you, why worry about the stars?'

—Tunisian proverb

*I*n order to understand the meaning of this proverb, you first need to understand the power of the full moon.

'Every 28 days when the Sun, Earth, and Moon are all aligned, a full moon occurs, and the Moon's surface is fully illuminated by the reflection of the Sun's light' (Hocken 2020). On this day, the Moon has completed its cycle and is at the height of its power. As we are deeply connected to not only the Earth, but to the Sun and Moon as well, we are also aligned and at the height of our powers during this time. Did you know that the Moon controls the ocean tides, and when a full moon occurs, the tides are much higher than usual? Did you know that the tidal effect of the Moon on Earth is more than twice as strong as that of the Sun (Hocken, Bikos and Jones 2020)? We, as humans, are made up of approximately 60% water, and just like the tide in the oceans, the Moon can have a major influence over us.

Many people have studied and followed the cycles of the Moon for centuries, and they understand that the full moon is the representation of completion and wholeness, an ending of a phase, a time to reflect on all they have achieved, release all that no longer serves their journeys, and prepare for the next phase.

As the full moon represents many things, the love of the full moon, in this instance, can represent the love from a partner, a feeling that everything is working in your favour, a feeling of contentment or completion within oneself, or even the love of God. Whatever it is, the love of the full moon represents your being perfectly aligned mentally, physically, and spiritually, within the right place, or with the right person. The love shared between you and what the Moon may represent in your life has been something into which you have put your energy. It has been growing stronger and stronger every day, and the love is finally at the height of its power.

It is something I pray we all experience one day.

It is indeed possible, but you must have the strength and determination to ignore those who will hate, criticise, judge, or compare what they have experienced to you in the hope of putting you off. It includes those who will just not support your journey, plus life's many distractions and challenges that we all face on the day to day. Simply put, it is the stars that cause you to lose sight of the full moon and the love it has to offer.

At the end of the day, the decision lays in your hands. Just know that there will be a time in your life when you will experience this exact situation if you haven't already. You can take a leap of faith and choose to receive the love of the full moon and experience something powerful, unique, and true, or you can allow yourself to be distracted by the stars, a cluster of balls of gas, that do not have your best intentions at heart and cannot offer the love you deserve.

Choose wisely.

Affirmation: I am worthy of love and deserve to receive love in abundance.

Lesson 6

---❖---

'Before healing others, heal yourself.'

—Gambian proverb

*I*f you are someone who constantly puts the needs of others before your own, it is time to stop.

It is time to put yourself first.

It is time to heal yourself first.

Most importantly, it is time to love yourself first.

Understand that putting yourself first does not mean you do not care about others—it simply means that you are wise enough to know that you cannot help others if you do not help yourself first.

Many of us are, in fact, broken, wounded, covered in cuts and bruises, be it figuratively or literally, as we have yet to heal from past traumas. These traumas live on in our minds and resurface once in a while to taunt us. They are the traumas that have completely changed us, the traumas that took away the light, our innocence, confidence, hope, love, and peace of mind. Just because you cannot see these wounds does not mean they are not there. I know you feel them constantly weeping and opening back up, but you hardly take the time to sit down and identify from where the wound has come, clean and disinfect it, sew it together, and cover it up to protect until it is fully healed.

It seems simple enough, but many of us have yet to do this.

However, for some reason, we always manage to find time for others. We happily clean and take care of their wounds, we heal them, we are listening ears, shoulders to cry on, support systems for our friends, family, parents, coworkers, and even acquaintances. We do this no matter the time, place, or person, yet we cannot find a day, or even an hour to spend with ourselves, work on ourselves, and heal ourselves.

Healing oneself from trauma is not an easy process. It takes time and patience, but it is absolutely necessary.

When you do not heal yourself and suppress your traumas, your mind gets stuck in the negative moments, and you will continue to relive the trauma, all the pain, emotions, and fear until you actively make a change. There are many ways you can begin your healing process, some more challenging than others, some more expensive, even some more taboo, such as counselling, hypnotherapy, meditation, rituals, churches, temples, affirmations, mindfulness, or speaking to elders…the list goes on. Also note that what works for some might not work for you, and vice versa, so it is important to do some research on different methods first, but your journeys will all start the same, with you admitting that you have wounds that need your time and attention to heal.

With every wound you heal, you will find a newfound sense of freedom and identity. You will be greater, stronger, wiser, and more in touch with yourself than you were before.

With every wound you heal, a weight of pain will be lifted from your shoulders, and you will feel so much lighter and happier. Your mind will be free and clear of clutter, creating space for more positive memories to live. With every wound you heal, you will learn to forgive those who have hurt you in the past, you will learn to forgive yourself and let go of all those toxic thoughts and feelings. Most importantly, you will learn to love yourself unapologetically and wholeheartedly. With every wound you heal, you will find a lesson to be learnt and shared to prevent yourself and others from making the same mistakes, which is the true key to healing others.

Take some time now to identify the wounds that need your immediate attention. This is the start of your healing process.

Affirmation: I owe myself the time, love, and attention
I give to other people.

PS Change the 'you' into 'I' in the last paragraph ('With every wound I heal') and say it out loud once a day to speak your healing into existence.

Lesson 7

———◆◦◆———

'When a person is not as she used to be, she does not behave as she used to behave.'

—Igbo proverb

C hange is inevitable.

Change is constant.

Change is necessary.

Every time an opportunity occurs for you to change, embrace it. At that moment, you have been provided with an opportunity to leave your past self, your foolish self, your naive self, your broken self, your negative self, and/or your old self behind.

In your lifetime, you will go through many changes and transitions, all of which are crucial for your development, growth, and life's journey. We all go through a biological change known as puberty when our childhood bodies change and develop as we transition into adolescence and adulthood.

As you grow older, many more changes follow: you change the way you think, who you socialise with, how you look, where you work, where you live, your partners...the list goes on.

Some changes are planned, and some are unexpected. Some changes are painful, and some are easy. Some people will criticise you whilst others will support you. Some changes you will not understand, and some you will welcome openly.

You may not realise the benefits within or reason behind moments of change and transition, but either way, they all provide you with an opportunity to learn more about yourself and the world around you. These changes will also push you out of your comfort zone and open a space in which you can grow into a new, better version of yourself.

Now, take a moment to reflect.

Reflect on all the changes and transitions through which you have been in your life so far: the small changes, the big changes, the good changes, and the difficult changes. Did you embrace these changes, or did you resist them?

Think of how these changes affected you (positively or negatively). Think of the lessons you learnt, and how they made you into the person you are today.

Looking back, do you now understand why these changes were necessary?

Some people in this world do not embrace the opportunity to change, learn, grow, or be a better version of themselves. This could be due to a fear of uncertainty, a lack of control, a negative past experience, a lack of confidence, or being comfortable or stuck in a habit. Some people are ultimately content with being just as they are, but the reality is that change is an inevitable force, and it will happen whether you like it or not. By refusing to change on your own accord, you will become trapped in the moment, stuck in your foolish, naïve, old self.

By rolling with the changes, you will continue to grow, and you will no longer be as you used to be or behave how you used to behave. You will create a better you.

> 'The secret of change is to focus all your energy, not fighting the old, but building the new.'
>
> —Socrates

Affirmation: Today, I will let go of the past I do not need and create the future I want.

Lesson 8

———◦│◦———

'The words of the night are coated with butter; as soon as the sun shines, they melt away.'

—Egyptian proverb

*T*hey say the best conversations happen late at night, and from my experience, I believe this to be true. There is something about those late-night conversations, a feeling that I, myself, am struggling to explain in words, but I know you understand what I mean.

I am talking about those late-night conversations that were not planned, where you stay up talking for hours about anything and everything that comes to your mind. You can feel your eyes getting heavy, but you ignore it because you are both so drawn into the conversation.

Those late-night conversations, where you make sure you are not talking too loudly, so you do not disturb anyone else in the house who is trying to sleep. You both take the time to express the deepest parts of yourself and reveal things that you do not usually reveal on a normal day, simply because you trust that person to hold your truths and secrets. Those late-night conversations are the ones you do not want to end, but you know that as soon as the sun comes up, the moment of calmness and closeness will melt away.

Whether it is on the phone or in-person with a friend, a partner, a sibling, a confidant, or maybe even a secret lover, there is something about those late-night conversations that cannot be compared to normal, daytime chit chat. The night itself provides ambient darkness, a feeling of warmth, safety, and openness, which is a complete contrast to what the night is usually associated with: danger, evil, and fear. Instead, it brings about a feeling of peace, vulnerability, openness, comfort, stillness, and freedom from stress or worry. The world around you is silent, and some of you can finally remove the masks you use during the day to hide your true selves.

Take a moment to reflect and think of the last late-night conversation you had. Think about the person you were talking to and about all the things you spoke. Think about how the conversation made you feel—were you able to express yourself freely? Think about how the conversation ended—did one of you fall asleep or did you talk until the sun came up? What happened after the conversation had ended?

The unfortunate thing about these late-night conversations is that they have to end. We cannot stay in that moment of tranquility, vulnerability, and peace forever as the morning is inevitable. The sunshine melts away the moment, some of you will put your masks back on to protect yourself from the harshness of the world outside, and all you are left with is the memory of the conversation, the feeling, and the person to whom you were speaking. It is a harsh reality, but there is always a silver lining and a lesson to be learnt from everything we experience, whether good or bad.

With every proverb there are many interpretations and lessons to be learnt, and you may be wondering what the lesson is within this situation. You see, there is something about a late-night conversation that is a form of therapy in itself. As your mind relaxes and your guard drops it provides an opportunity for your subconscious to open up and reveal everything: your deepest fears, your regrets, your insecurities, your fantasies, what makes you happy, what makes you sad, your ideals, your career path, your relationships, your past, your present, your future, your everything!

So, the next time, before the sun shines, before the moment has melted away, and before you step out into the world, take the time to write a few notes during these late-night conversations, be it mental or physical, as your internal voice is speaking and expressing all you need to know about yourself. As well, areas within yourself on which you need to work/heal are being highlighted.

Most importantly, find the person with which to have these meaningful, late-night conversations so you can help each other to release, learn, and grow.

Affirmation: I now release all unwanted thoughts and emotions that prevent me from connecting to my inner-self.

Lesson 9

'Life is like ballet performance, danced only once.'

—Malian proverb

*B*allet is an art form like no other. It is a highly technical, unique form of storytelling through the use of dance. 'Where the performer uses their body to speak, express emotion, and engage the audience with the most intricate and skilled movements' (Wensjoe 2020). It requires performers to be wholeheartedly in tune with their minds, bodies, and spirits. A lot of skill, time, hard work, and dedication goes into a ballet performance. The performers have to ignore any external noises that could hinder their performance. They must be confident, trust themselves with every move, and learn from any mistakes they have made in the past. During the dance, performers flow with the highs and lows of the narrative and allow themselves to feel and express every emotion.

A ballet performance is very similar to the way you move through your life.

Firstly, the Creator has provided you with a unique costume made of the finest materials and a set of tailored shoes that fit you and only you. Unfortunately for this performance called life, you cannot practice or rehearse until you get it perfect, but know that you have already been provided with the skills and talent you need. You just have to learn to trust yourself, be confident, and be in tune with your mind, body, and spirit, and you will unlock all you need to have a successful performance. Understand that what you experience each day—the highs, the lows, and everything in between—is an intricate part of the performance of life and a part of the narrative. Learn to embrace and flow with each moment, movement, and emotion as it is all a part of your life's journey.

It is important to note that this is not a solo performance. You may have been cast as the lead role, but you still have your supporting cast to pick you up and raise you higher. They are also there to offer a helping hand to help you transition around the stage. Most importantly, they are there to catch you when you fall. Similarly, in life, your friends, family, partners, teachers, coworkers, and sometimes, even strangers provide you with the support, feedback, and guidance you need to help you. Take note of these people in your life, and do not be afraid to reach to and ask for help when you need it.

Within many ballet performances and narratives, the main character, or protagonist, is always challenged by a villain or antagonist who serves as an obstacle they must struggle to overcome. You will—or you might have already—come across a few people like this in your life who refuse to support you or judge every move you make. Like the trained professionals, you must learn to ignore any external noise that might affect your performance and focus your attention and energy on yourself. This is your performance, your one chance to show the world who you are—do not waste your energy on people who do not serve your purpose as there are no redos.

The spotlight has always been on you. Your stage has been prepared from birth, and your performance has been great so far. You may have had a few stumbles and missed steps, but do not worry: it happens. The villain threw you off a bit, and you may have lost your focus, but fortunately, your supporting cast caught you in time. With everything in life, there is room for improvement, and I know that you have yet to express yourself truly.

Remember that this is your one dance, there are no practices, no rehearsals, and no re-dos, so before you reach the final act, make sure you have shown the world all you have to offer. You still have time.

Take a deep breath.

Trust yourself.
Dance!

Affirmation: This life is mine to enjoy, and it is up to me to do so.

Lesson 10

———•◦•———

'One must talk little and listen a lot.'

—Mauritania proverb

*D*id you know that the most powerful instrument in your possession right now is your voice?

At this moment in time, there are approximately 7.8 billion people in the world who also possess this power. Approximately 7.8 billion people with their own thoughts, opinions, critiques, and stories to share, who all have the right to freedom of speech and the right to express all they feel to the world.

Now, some people use this power to spread words of encouragement, love, peace, and most importantly, positivity. Their words are carefully thought out and delivered with the intention to uplift, help, and inspire those around them.

There are those who may abuse their power to spread words of hate, destruction, lies, and worst of all, negativity, without taking into consideration what they are saying or how their words will affect the people receiving them. It is important to understand that your words are an extremely powerful energy, as from words alone, the world in which we live was spoken into existence. If used correctly, you can manifest many wonderful things into existence through your words, such as love, happiness, peace of mind, success, wealth, and the like.

You must learn to understand that every word you speak is as important as the last. How you consistently speak about yourself and others, be it positive or negative, will be manifested into reality, whether you like it or not.

So, if you choose to speak words of hate, criticism, complaint, or negativity towards yourself, it will become your reality, and if you do the same to others, you will hinder theirs. It is important to note that people's words can also affect your reality; it is not a one-way thing. You may have already noticed how a simple, negative comment from a friend, family member, or coworker can ruin your day in comparison to a positive comment. So, it is important to surround yourself and only engage with positive people, so you can uplift each other collectively.

This is why words should be carefully thought out and prepared before they are released into the world. Of course, this is easier said than done. Once you learn to think before you speak, you may find yourself questioning your choice of words and whether they provide sustenance or value to yourself, others, or the world at large.

The next time you open your mouth to speak, ask yourself these five questions:

1. Why am I about to say this?
2. Is it positive?
3. Is it helpful?
4. Is it necessary?
5. Can silence provide the answer?

In this world, everyone has the right to speak freely, but it does not mean you should. You must learn to keep a closed mouth and open your ears and eyes. Through the silence, you can see, hear, and learn more about yourself, others, and the world around you. Then, you can decide if the words you wish to release into the world are necessary.

Affirmation: Today, I practice the skill of being quiet.
I will open my ears and listen.

Lesson 11

*'Unless you call out, who will
open the door?'*

—Ethiopian proverb

*W*hy do we find it so hard to ask for help when we need it?

Why do we sit and contemplate every possible option before asking for help?

Why are we willing to help others but cannot ask for help for ourselves?

I, myself, have been guilty of this and understand there are many reasons as to why people do not like the idea of asking for help.

Whether it is the fear of being rejected by the person you asked for help, or the fear of being seen as a failure or incompetent, the fear of owing someone, the fear of depending on others, or of being judged, a negative past experience, or simply your pride is what stops you from being vulnerable and asking for help.

Everyone has their own reasons as to why they do not like asking for help; however, by not asking for help, you inevitably block your progress and development. You will be stuck in a cycle of needing help but not asking for it until you reach the breaking point, and in the end, you will have no choice but to ask for help.

You need to understand that the same energy and support you have given to others should be expected and welcomed back. Help is always at hand in every situation, so there is no need to suffer in silence.

There are billions of people in this world, and each person has their own set of unique skills, talents, and abilities, but there is not a single person in the world who can do everything, carry every load, or harness every skill and ability—it is impossible. Why put that burden on yourself?

There are many things you can do that others cannot, and there are many things others can do that you cannot.

So, when you are in a situation where you need help, understand the following:

The first person you ask may not be able to help you, so have the courage to ask someone else. You will find the right person in the end. Note that there will be things you do not know or understand, but life is about learning and growing. The people around you can teach many valuable lessons if you just ask for help.

Understand that it is a natural instinct for people to help others, and most people are more than willing to do so. Everyone needs a shoulder to lean on from time to time, and even the most independent people have a support system and mentors to whom they can go to ask for help and advice. It is okay to try to figure things out on your own, but if you have tried and failed, then it is time for you to seek help and guidance from another source. At some stage in everyone's lives, they have had to ask for help—you are not alone, and no one can judge you. There is nothing wrong with being proud and having pride in yourself, but if your pride blocks your progress, then simply push it to the side and ask for help.

If you fear asking people for help in general, remember that there is someone you can call for help that is guaranteed to answer. Turn to God, the Creator, or the universe, as you refer to it, who will give you the strength and courage to ask for help and provide you with the right people to guide and support you.

I have spoken about manifesting things into existence and in your life before, so if you need help, all you have to do is open your mouth, ask, and your request will be heard.

Ask for help when you need it. Call out, and the right people will hear you. They will help you open the door, but if you do not, you will be left stuck behind that door forever, waiting and blaming others for not helping.

Affirmation: I ask for help when I need it. I am open and ready to receive all that I need.

Lesson 12

---◆◆◆---

*'Better building bridges than
building walls.'*

—Swahili proverb

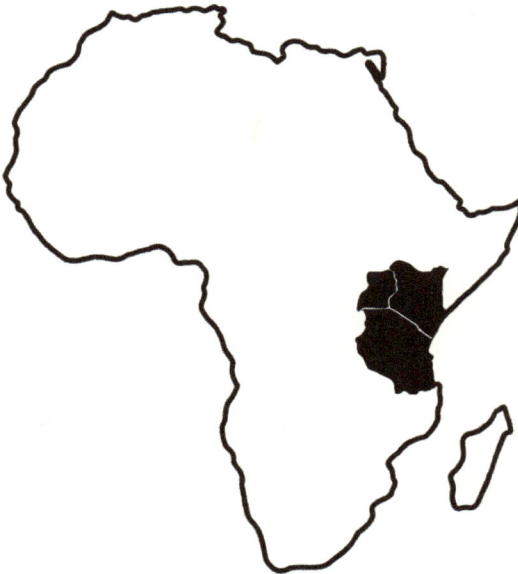

Apparently, there are approximately 'four hundred fifty-three billion, two hundred seventy-six million, seven hundred and eighty-four thousand, three hundred and twenty-six bridges in the world' (Andersen 2017). If you did not grasp how many bridges that is, maybe you should read it again. If you did, then you know that is a lot of bridges!

That is four hundred fifty-three billion, two hundred seventy-six million, seven hundred and eighty four thousand, three hundred and twenty six different ways that people can connect with one another, travel, and transport goods.

To put it in perspective, out of these billions of bridges in the world, thirty-five of them are based in London, and I, myself, am within walking distance from at least three of these.

Did you know that the Arkadiko Bridge or Kazarma Bridge located in Greece is 'one of the oldest arch bridges, which dates back to the bronze ages and is still in existence and in use today' (Johnson 2020)? Did you know that the Danyang-Kunshan Grand Bridge, located between Shanghai and Nanjing in Jiangsu province, 'is the longest bridge in the world at 102.4 miles long' (Gammon 2020)? You learn something new every day.

The fact that there are so many bridges in the world highlights their importance within our lives on the day to day. The purpose of a bridge is to allow people or vehicles to cross from one end to another or to connect one place to another.

Like most things in life, there is always a deeper meaning; for some people, a bridge represents a link, connection, freedom, journeying into the unknown, a path, a decision, relationships, unity, opportunity, progress, stability, transition, or hope.

Take a moment to think about what the symbol of a bridge means to you.

Building a bridge requires a lot of hands, resources, dedication, precision, and skill to piece together every element to form a functional and unique design. It is a timely process that can take anywhere between days and years to construct, but the results prove it is worth the time and effort as a bridge can last for hundreds of years, connecting many generations of people and locations. I suggest that, after you finish reading this, you go online to type in 'How bridges are built', as I will not be able to explain with my mere words alone. You will see for yourself the amazing process of building a bridge.

When life gets hard, people may hurt us, or things do not go the way we planned, many of us are quick to build a wall or remove people from our lives and put up our guard as a form of protection. Now, there is nothing wrong with building a wall as there are times when everyone's intentions are not pure, but building a wall without considering a bridge first is where the problem lies. Like the bridge, a wall has a deeper meaning, too: 'walls are definite things, immovable and strong' (Jones 2019). What you may see as protection, safety, or home, others see as a blockage, barrier, or even entrapment. When you build walls, it is not just because of the negative people or bad experiences you are blocking out—it is everyone and everything. You are surrounded by walls every day, they are the first things you see when you wake up, you are surrounded by them at work, school, and for some, mentally. You must understand that a wall is a short-term fix, and you will eventually have to break it down when you want to move on or move forward.

It is important to note that it takes just as much work and effort to build a bridge as it does a wall, so look for where you can build bridges!

Building a bridge requires more than one pair of hands, so how about you start on one end, and I will start on the other. We can take our time putting each piece down to meet in the middle. When we finish, we will be standing on mutual ground, and we can figure out this journey through life together. Our bridge will connect two worlds together to allow many generations of people to cross, connect, teach, learn, and explore.

See how easy it was to build a bridge? Now, it is time for you to build another!

Affirmation: I allow myself to change. I am open to a new way of being.

Lesson 13

'A person always breaking off from work never finishes anything.'

—**Nigerian proverb**

*T*he art of procrastination.

I call it an art form because it takes pure skill and mastery to continually convince yourself that you deserve a break when you have not actually done much work in the first place.

The funny thing is that you know exactly what work you need to do. You have planned everything out, step by step, and you most likely have a deadline, yet you still have not found the motivation to get started.

Procrastination is the 'avoidance of completing specific tasks that need to be accomplished by a certain deadline' (Duff 2016). Some examples include everyday household chores, homework, assignments, making important appointments, submitting applications, or even having a needed or difficult conversation with someone.

Many of us come up with excuses such as 'I'm too tired', 'I'm waiting for inspiration', 'I'll do it later', 'I'm waiting for the right moment', 'I won't be able to finish it on time', or 'It's not that important', 'I'll do it another day', 'after this episode, I'll start', 'I'm waiting for help', 'I work well under pressure', or 'I'm just going to have a quick break'— sound familiar?

In all honesty, the list goes on and on and on. Over the years, I, myself, have created a list of excuses not to do something, and the distraction of social media does not help, either. Procrastination is something that affects a lot of people in their day to day lives, so you are not alone.

Take a moment to reflect on the times you procrastinated.

What excuses did you make?

How many times did you miss an important deadline?

Was that moment of procrastination worth it?

It is important to understand that procrastination is not necessarily bad or wrong.

However, the problem that arises is when you take constant breaks or prolong a task to the point of completely avoiding it, especially when you know there may be a consequence or outcome for this action. This type of passive procrastination can be caused by a number of things, such as fear of failing. Some people believe that if they do not start something in the first place, they cannot fail. They can save themselves the stress and energy of completing a difficult task, and focus on things that are easier to achieve. Also, a lack of focus—some people are not able to keep their end date in sight or stick to the goals they set out for themselves.

Striving for perfection is another example. Some people set their standards too high and have a fear of not being able to reach them, so they continually put something off until they can do it 'perfectly'. Another reason is the fear of what is next. Some people may feel that when they finish one task, another one will pop up that will be even more difficult, so by intentionally avoiding the current task, they will not have to deal with whatever is next in line. You need to understand that all of these excuses allow procrastination to take over and will ultimately result in a build-up of unfinished work, which will have to be completed eventually. So, it is time to break this habit!

It is important to note that your mind and body often need time to rest, think, and reset, so it is okay for you to take a few breaks here and there, focus your attention on other things, and/or delay a task for a day or two, as long as you have the motivation to return to the task to get it completed on time. Know that you can actively procrastinate, which means you allow your mind to wander, but you are still in control and are able to get things done without any fear or doubt blocking your progress.

Below are a few tips to help you work proactively alongside your procrastination:

- Make a plan and break down your task step by step. Include dates, times, and an outline of what you need to achieve.
- Set yourself daily reminders and realistic goals that you MUST achieve before the next day.
- Give yourself a timeframe for when it needs to be 100% complete (I recommend a day before the actual deadline).
- Find out the time of day at which you work best and schedule your work around that time.
- Avoid distractions, put your phone on 'do not disturb' for 30 minutes to an hour, find a quiet space in which to work. You can even ask people in your household to give you some quiet time to focus.
- Ask for help when you need it! If you do not understand what is expected of you or you need assistance, ask your team members, friends, family, or others.
- Schedule in your break. Work solidly for 45-50 minutes and break for ten to 15 minutes maximum. You can use an alarm to help.

***Affirmation: I am focused, determined, and I will never quit.
I will achieve all of my goals.***

FYI: This was your tea break, so get back to work and complete your tasks. This book will still be here when you have finished!

Lesson 14

'It is not what you call me, but what I answer to.'

—**African proverb**

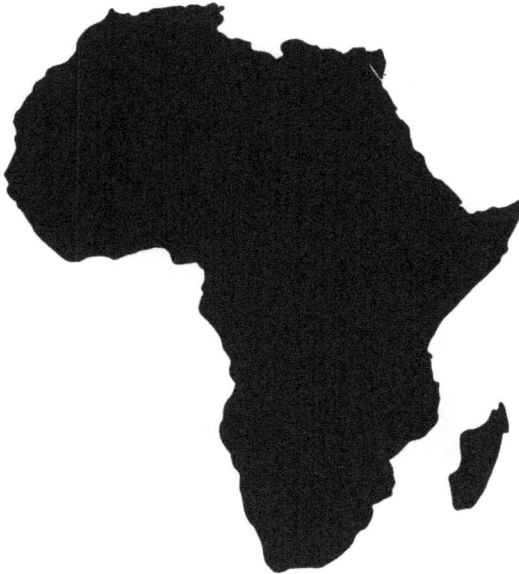

*T*he fastest way to remove someone's identity, humanity, and spirit is to strip away their name.

This is the unfortunate fate my ancestors experienced with the invasion of the Europeans on the continent of Africa when countless numbers of African men, women, and children were stolen from their homes and made into slaves across Europe and the Americas. The first thing the white slave masters did once they bought and branded said Africans, was to have their African names removed and changed.

Some were given European names, such as 'Mary', 'John', or 'Joseph', whilst others were simply called 'Slave 1-2-3', 'boy/girl', and worst of all, 'nigger', a word that is still actively used in today's society. This was done to strip the African people of their identity, culture, language, customs, and humanity, and we see the major effects of this action today, as a loss of identity, language, culture, and traditions still plagues some Black people in the diaspora and on the continent.

Some of our names were carefully planned out and chosen by our parents, grandparents, or elders. For others, their names may have been decided after they were born, changed at the last minute, or decided completely on a whim. Some of us may have more than one name, whilst others only have one. Either way, they are our names, our identities, and our power.

It is important to understand that every name has its unique meaning and gives us an understanding of who we are and our purpose on this earth. We must stop allowing people to call us by something other than our names, mispronounce, or tarnish them in any way.

When we refer back to traditional African teachings and practices, naming ceremonies are seen as highly important when a child is born. Every country has its own naming ceremonies and special days to name a child. For some countries, the ceremony is held on the day of the child's birth, the day after, or even a week later. A child's name is carefully chosen by an elder, parent, or grandparent and can also be decided based on the circumstances in which the child was born (Sogoba 2019). Within Africa, there is a strong belief that your name is a direct link to your soul. When a child is blessed with a name, it is for both their physical and spiritual bodies. Your name sets out your life's path and highlights your journey to earth and the journey upon which you will embark on earth (OriginsInfo 2017). This is why most countries give their children two names: their destiny name, which is said to come from the heavens and/or spiritual realm, meant to be protected and not shared with everyone, and the assumed name, which is given by an elder or family member on earth.

So, to future parents reading this: please take time when deciding your child's name.

Your names are a gift and a true representation of who you are, your identity, and your individuality. It does not matter if someone has the same name as you; the energy, power, and spirit within your name is different.

Your name adds value to your existence, reaffirms your humanity, allows people to recognise and connect with you. Unfortunately, we live in a society where people make assumptions about your character based on your name.

If a name is too hard to pronounce, people might avoid communication, give you a nickname (without your permission) to make it easier for them, or assume you are a difficult person, overall. If your name is not a traditional Western name, some people will assume you are not on their level of communication, or overall standards, and will, most likely, look down on you, but if your name is a traditional Western name—such as 'Sarah Smith', but you are black—it can still have a negative response. There are many examples of this, and I am sure many of you can remember a time when someone incorrectly pronounced your name without the intention to correct it or ask for the right pronunciation, mistreated you because of your name, or called you by a completely different name.

Here are some words of advice.

When someone incorrectly pronounces your name, correct them straight away. Say it loudly, boldly, and say it only once. Once is more than enough, and if they continue to incorrectly pronounce it, do not answer them until they do.

When someone mistreats you because of your name or calls you by a different name, do not respond. When you know your name, what it means, and the power it possesses, there is no need to respond to people who are being disrespectful and ignorant.

If they do not call you by your name, do not answer.

Take a look at my name. I am Kesi Steven. This is my full name. I do have a middle name, but for the sake of tradition, it must remain protected.

Each of my names has its own meaning, and as a collective, highlights who I am, my journey to earth, and the journey on which I am currently embarking.

Kesi is my given name, chosen by my mum, and it means born when her father was working hard or in a time of difficulty, which was, in fact, true.

My middle/destiny name was chosen by my dad, and it is the path I am on.

Steven is my family name, given to my ancestors during slavery by the slave master. It highlights my Caribbean heritage and the history of my family.

You may call me Kesi, Kesi Steven, or Miss Steven. These are the only names to which I will answer, and I have had to correct people many times throughout my life (even though my name is only four letters long), but I am proud of my name, I respect my name, and understand its meaning. With every move I make, I put more power into my name, so when the time comes for me to pass, my name will mean so much more.

To you, the reader—take the time to answer these questions:

What is your name?

Who gave you your name?

What does your name mean?

Most importantly, to what name do you answer?

Affirmation: I will not let anyone take away my identity, my individuality, or my spirit. I am confident within myself, and I know the power I possess.

Lesson 15

'*Absence makes the heart forget.*'

—**African proverb**

They say that absence makes the heart grow fonder. Apparently, when there is a physical distance between two people, their affection and love grow stronger. It is a beautiful sentiment, but this is not the truth. Absence, indeed, makes the heart grow fonder when there is still a strong, consistent form of communication and connection between you and the other person. Even if that person is not physically there, you can still communicate via phone calls, texts, emails, letters, and visit whenever you can.

When someone leaves and the communication and connection ceases to exist, so does our love and fondness. When it comes to love, our hearts play a vital role in how we feel, express, and experience different emotions. Throughout history, the two have been linked together, and science has proven that the heart is more than just an organ that pumps blood through your body. It also responds when we experience specific emotions such as sadness, thoughtfulness, excitement, anxiety, love, and fear.

So, what happens to our hearts when someone leaves us?

When someone we deeply care for abandons us, it can leave what feels like a large gaping hole within our hearts that seems like it will never be filled again. Many, if not all of us, have experienced the hurt and pain of someone leaving and the struggle to understand how and why this person can walk away from us so easily. Whether it was a parent who abandoned you at a young age, a close friend who cut you off unexpectedly, a partner who broke up with you, or a lover who ghosted you, this is something that many people can relate to, so you are not alone. Although everyone's experiences are different, we have all felt that aching pain in the centre of our hearts, that sick feeling in the pits of our stomachs, the daily fight with our eyes not to cry, and the battle in our minds that over-analyses everything and is ready to forget and move on, though our hearts are broken, and we are not ready.

I apologise if I have triggered you to make you remember the feeling or a moment like this, but with everything I write, there is a lesson to learn and a message I have to share.

It is important to understand that if you do not take the time to heal your heart, the pain of some absences can leave you feeling hurt for a lifetime.

As time passes, the reality of the person not coming back or not having given you a reason as to why s/he left in the first place begins to set in. Some people allow their broken hearts to continue to guide them, and they end up dwelling in the pain and loneliness. Others will look elsewhere to fill the void, which can all lead to even more hurt. When something is broken, it is damaged, it does not work, and it needs time to repair and/or heal; therefore, listening to or being guided by a broken heart will only cause you to become even more broken.

Would you still use a broken alarm clock and trust it to wake you up for work in the morning?

No, I did not think so.

Instead, you must listen to your mind—specifically, your intuition, that little voice in your head—which will guide you and tell you what you need to heal. All you have to do is listen. Your intuition is like that friend who pushes you to get your sh!t together, who tells you the truth even when you do not want to hear it, who does not take no for an answer, who wants to see you win, and who will make you understand that you must always put yourself and your needs first. Only then will the real healing begin, and if there will be no more pain, sadness, or loneliness, that gaping hole will be replaced and filled with self-love, peace of mind, and optimism. In time, your heart will forget the feeling of love and emotional attachment you once had for that person. The memory of them may still live on in your mind, and you may reflect on it once in a while, and this is okay as long as you do not dwell too long in these negative feelings.

Everything in life is a cycle of many beginnings and many endings. People come and go—this is a natural part of life's journey. As the saying goes, some people are here for a reason, some people are here for a season, and some people are here for a lifetime. Learn to enjoy each moment and keep your heart open to love in any form. Do not worry about it getting broken as you have the knowledge and strength to protect and heal yourself.

If they are in your life for a reason, understand that it will be a short stay, but they will have an important lesson to teach you, and once you identify what the lesson is you can let go and move on peacefully. If they are in your life for a season, understand there is something you both need to experience, and once you have experienced all you can, it is okay to let go and move on peacefully. If they are in your life for a lifetime, then you have nothing to worry about or fear—the love is everlasting, so embrace every moment of it.

Affirmation: Today, I choose to heal my heart, mind, body and spirit. I forgive myself and those who have hurt me in the past. My heart may be broken, but I will fill each crack with all the love I have to offer.

Lesson 16

—————•◦•—————

'The words of the elders become sweet someday.'

—Malawian proverb

*T*his book is evidence enough that the words of our elders may become sweet and important one day.

We are just over halfway through these lessons and have learnt so much already. These proverbs have taught you about self-worth, peace of mind, listening, being optimistic, knowing your power, and so much more. There are so many lessons to be learnt from African proverbs alone, so imagine all the other gems of wisdom our elders have been trying to tell us over the years.

Within the African tradition, an elder is like an overseer for a community. They ensure that traditions and customs are followed and practised properly. They maintain order amongst the people within the community and have the final say in every meeting (Africa: Age and Aging 2020).

Elders also ensure there is peace and balance between the people and the land. They teach youth within the community by instilling values and morals. Elders also perform initiations and connect people with their ancestors. Most importantly, they work in harmony with God and protect God's creations.

The status of the elder is not synonymous with age. In order to become an elder, one has to go through multiple rites of passage/initiations from birth to old age, highlighting the serious responsibility of this role, its importance to the community, and the level of respect an elder has. Due to colonisation and influences from Western social structures, the roles of elders and their authority have changed over time.

The role of an elder differs for those of us in the diaspora as some customs and traditions have been lost, abandoned, or changed throughout the generations. In this regard, an elder can be synonymous with age; therefore, an elder is usually a grandparent, uncle, aunt, or someone within the extended family or wider community. They aren't chosen, they have not gone through any specific rites of passage/

initiations, and there is less emphasis on their authority as elders, as listening to what they have to say is more a choice than an obligation.

I say 'choice' as when we were younger or even now, many of us have the same reaction when our elders approach us. Whether at home, in the streets, at family functions, or in a phone call, as soon as the conversation begins, that voice in our head says, 'Ahh, man—here comes the lecture.' Our minds are so focused on our escape plans that we do not appreciate what is being said to us at that moment.

The funny thing about conversations with our elders is that when we do decide to listen, they can end in one of two ways. You either leave the conversation with a handful of keywords of advice, gain more knowledge and understanding of the world in which we live, and a deeper sense of self, or 15 minutes into the conversation, you realise your elder is, in fact, rambling on and on about nothing. You try to make sense of what they are saying, you may have even planned your escape route, but the voice in your head lets you know it is impolite for you to walk away mid-ramble, so you just have to listen anyway.

Take a moment now to think about who you consider an elder in the traditional meaning described above. Think about how often you listen to them and how often you do not. Think about the times their words alone have helped you get through some tough situations, or when they have taught you something new.

It is important to understand that your elders have a lot more experience than you do. They have been through all of the ups and downs life's journey has to offer. Your elders have pushed through and overcome many challenges, some that you may never have to face yourself. Over the years, they have gained more knowledge and understanding of how the world works, who they are within the world, and how to live life. All of the knowledge and wisdom they have gained can then be passed on to you, to help you navigate life's journey. All you have to do is listen.

Remember that our elders have lived a life without us, but we have never lived a life without them. They sometimes know us more than we know ourselves, and they are prepared and willing to take on the role of your teacher, supporter, and counsellor. Whether you agree or disagree with what is being said, always take the time to listen. The words may not benefit you at the present moment, but they may in the future. I understand that some people like to figure things out on their own, but you do not have to put that pressure on yourself. Just know that help and support are there when you need it, so, the next time you are struggling, need advice, or feel lost, look to your elders. Seek them out rather than wait for them to come. Finally, listen to their sweet words of reassurance and knowledge.

The time may come when you are considered an elder, and all you have learnt in life can be used to sweeten the path of the next generation. So, learn from the words of those who came before, and reassure those that come after you learn from yours.

Affirmation: I am fully present and listen intently when elders speak.

Lesson 17

---•◦•---

'If you want to lean on a tree, first make sure it can hold you.'

—Cameroonian proverb

*D*id you know that there are 'approximately [three] trillion trees in the world and of those [three] trillion there are 60 different species of trees' (Kornei 2017)? Symbolically speaking, a tree can represent protection, strength, healing, connection, spirituality, exploration, the unseen, fertility, grounding, transformation, power, or growth. This differs depending on the country, as each culture has its own symbolism and connection to trees.

The beautiful thing about trees is that each individual tree has its own meaning—an oak tree represents strength, longevity and nobility; a birch tree represents beginnings, renewal, and youth; a holly tree represents action, assertion, and objectivity; an elder tree represents transition, evolution and continuation; a willow tree— which is my favourite tree—represents imagination, intuition, life, and vision.

The most important thing to understand about this is that each tree is different.

Each type of tree has its own unique characteristics, energy, and symbology; therefore, not all trees can offer you the same 'support'. For example, if you are looking for strength and power, you would not lean on a willow tree; you would seek out an oak tree.

If you are looking for a change and something new, you would not lean on an oak tree, you would seek out an elder tree. So, when you are in need of a specific type of support, you have to learn to choose the tree accordingly.

It sounds simple enough, but some people do not consider whether or not the tree can hold them. They just assume it can because it looks strong, it has always been there or has supported them in the past, thus, causing more harm to the tree as well themselves, as they, too, can end up falling along with the damaged tree.

In life, there will be times when you may feel lost, upset, scared, or hurt, and you look to your close friends for support, advice, to vent, or simply for someone on which to lean. Your friends are usually more than happy to be there for you, come rain or shine, but just like the trees, not every friend can hold you or offer the right type of support you need at the time.

Take a moment to think about your group of friends. Think about each individual person. You will notice that no one friend is exactly the same, and like the trees, they all have their unique characteristics, personalities, and energies.

Every friendship group is different, and the dynamics can change, so you may have that one friend who is always up for a good time and has a carefree outlook on life, or that friend who is quieter and laid back. There is also that wise friend who always has advice and keeps you in check or the funny friend who finds humour in everything and knows how to make you laugh. You may even have an emotional friend who is more compassionate, expressive, and sensitive.

When it comes to leaning on a friend for support, you must first take the following into consideration: sometimes your friends are not as strong as they seem. They may be dealing with their own personal struggles and may not have the mental strength at that moment in time to hold you up as well as themselves. It happens sometimes, and there will be moments when you have to push your needs to the side in order to make sure your friend is okay. Another point to take into consideration is that your friend may not be able to offer you the right advice or support. This could be due to a lack of knowledge or experience.

Sometimes your friends' characteristics may affect the type of support they can provide. For example, if a situation occurs where you need solid advice, you would not reach out to your more 'emotional' friend, as s/he may cause you to overreact and think with your heart rather than your head. Rather, you would seek out your 'wise' friend who can help you process and think logically.

If a situation occurs in which you need a pick me up, or a good time to forget about your troubles, you would not seek out your 'chill' friend on which to lean, as that could cause you to retreat within yourself and be introspective, causing you to overthink all of the what-ifs, whys, and hows. You should seek out your carefree friend, the one who knows exactly where to go to have a good time and allow you to be stress-free.

By not taking the time to choose the right friend, you may feel as if your needs are not being met or your friend simply does not care, causing more damage to your emotions, leaving the situation unresolved.

So, before leaning on a friend, make sure they can hold you first. Sending a simple text message or phone call asking your friends how they are and if they have a moment to listen to your needs can make a whole load of a difference. This will allow both of you to set aside some time to prepare yourself mentally for the conversation at hand. I say this not to dishearten you from reaching out to your friends when you are in need, but instead, to take some time to think about the situation as a whole and the specific support you need, so the right person can hold you up. Choosing the wrong friend to lean on could damage you both.

Affirmation: I love and care for my friends always. I will always support and uplift them as they support and uplift me.

Lesson 18

*'Love has to be shown by deeds,
not words.'*

—Swahili proverb

*W*hat is love?

I have been sitting here for the past two days, trying to write a single explanation for what love is, and in all honesty, I cannot.

Science tends to have this need for logical, rational explanations for anything and everything, but a simple Internet search will tell you that love is 'a mixture of many different emotions', 'an intense feeling', or 'a strong constant affection for someone' (GoodTherapy.org 2020), but I believe it is much more than that.

Love cannot be put into a box with labels on it. Love is an energy that is free to flow through anything and anyone. Love travels where it is called to go and where it is needed. Love is internal, external, and can be expressed in many different ways. Everyone has—or will have—their own experience with love, and sometimes we forget that love can come in many different forms: between partners, between a parent and a child, within a family, between friends, for oneself, for the earth, and for God.

This is why I say that a single description of love is impossible.

For the purpose of this lesson, love is simplified into an equation: a feeling + an action + a word—not necessarily in that order, but you must have all three equally balanced for it to be considered love. It is important to note that this can be applied for any form of love I mentioned previously.

The most significant part of this equation is the word 'balance'; it is the key to your being successful in love. We are a generation who is constantly bombarded with conceptions of 'struggle love' from external sources such as TV, social media, films, and those in our lives who like to project their versions and experiences of love. For example, we are told and shown that love is rare to find, conditional, destructive, abusive, fickle, feared, or unbalanced, but in reality, it is not the energy of love that is unbalanced; it is the person who is unbalanced and not aligned with the energy of love.

For most people today, one element of the equation is missing, so it is either that love is a feeling + a word - action, a word + action - the feelings, or action + feeling - the words—the equations aren't balanced. This highlights why many people feel like they are struggling when it comes to giving and receiving love in their day to day lives.

Take a moment now to think about what love means to you and what your definition of love is.

When it comes to love in its many forms, the feelings, the words, and the actions must be given the same level of importance and balanced equally.

Words will never be enough if the feeling is not there. You must first learn to nurture the feeling of love and allow it to grow over time. You must learn to be patient and take each feeling and moment as it comes.

Secondly, you must learn to open up your heart and allow yourself to receive love. Many people tend to be guarded in order to protect themselves from experiencing hurt or pain. Now, as I have said before, there is nothing wrong with having an initial guard to protect yourself—the issue is when you want to experience this love but refuse or cannot find the courage to take take it down. Whether that love brings you happiness or meets your worst fear, it adds to your life's experience. As the saying goes: 'tis better to have loved and lost, than to never have loved at all.'

Words will never be enough if the actions do not match. Love is not abusive, lonely, possessive, scary, or selfish, but a person can be. The act of loving is a skill in itself, something you will have to identify, learn, and apply in your everyday life. The daily act of loving has been broken down into five love languages:

1. Words of affirmation
2. Quality time
3. Gift receiving
4. Acts of service
5. Physical touch

Although many people tend to look at these five love languages in relation to romantic partnership, they can be applied to all forms of love. For example, you can learn to speak positive words of affirmation to your partner, children, self, friends, family, the earth, and God, or learn to spend quality time with your partner, children, self, friends, family, the earth, and God, and so on. As love is reciprocal, ensure you receive this in return.

No one has just one love language, but a combination of all five, so take the time to study yourself and the person who is receiving your love and know when to apply each one.

When you have an equal balance of feelings + words + actions, then you know it is real love. Anything other than this is a compromise. Love is an energy that is free to flow through anything and anyone. Love travels where it is called to go and where it is needed. Love is internal and external. Love can be found in many places, and the key to finding love—real love, true love—lies within.

Affirmation: I am love.

Lesson 19

'Leadership does not depend on age.'

—Namibian proverb

Simply put, leadership is defined as the ability to inspire and guide a group of people to achieve a common goal (Ward 2020). This can be applied in work, politics, activism, religion, school, family, and more.

Therefore, the concept of a 'leader' can be expressed through roles such as manager, teacher, mentor, parent, and activist. There are those who are born—or should I say, destined—to be leaders. They have the natural skills, qualities, and the charisma to take on a leadership role. There are also those who aspire to be leaders. They may not have the natural qualities, but they have the passion, determination, and a willingness to learn and work towards the role of 'leader'. Furthermore, there are those who are chosen as leaders, whether it is by the outside community who feel they are the best people to lead them or by a circumstance that forces them into that role.

You are surrounded by many leaders in your day-to-day life, some are good and highly respected whilst others are questionable, indeed. I am sure that you can identify both types of leaders within your life's journey and throughout world history.

Research states that to be a good leader, you must have the ability to speak with intention, encourage, support, have a clear vision, strategise, delegate tasks, lead by example, be integral, adapt, be empathetic, teach, communicate effectively, be self-aware, be respectful, be passionate, be decisive, and be humble, (CCL 2020)—notice how age wasn't mentioned!

Age is simply the indicator of how long your physical body has been on this earth, and it should not restrict or be used to measure one's ability to be or achieve anything.

Some of the world's greatest leaders have varied in age, from Nelson Mandela's becoming the oldest head of state in South Africa at 75 to Martin Luther King's spearheading and becoming a key figure in the civil rights movement from the age of 26. They are two key figures in history who spent the majority of their lives fighting for justice and equality. They brought communities together and led many people, but they were on opposite ends of the age spectrum.

In most recent times, we have had even younger leaders emerging, such as Zulaikha Patel who, at the age of 13, led a protest with her classmates against the school's ban on natural hair in 2016, demonstrating that leadership is not dependent on age but dependent on the person who possesses the true qualities of a leader in a given situation and time. So, whether you are born into leadership, aspire to leadership, or called into leadership, even if you think you are too young or too old, do not consider age as a barrier for making a change.

Affirmation: I have the power to create change.

Lesson 20

'Treat the days well, and they will treat you well.'

—Zambian proverb

*W*e all know the struggle of waking up on the wrong side of the bed and believing that a 'bad' day is soon to follow. It is as if the moment your foot leaves the bed a series of unexpected chaotic events occur, and you seem to have lost control of the whole day. Whether it is running late for work, a large stain on your clothes, missing the train, forgetting something important at home, stubbing your toe, a toilet mishap, a blister on the heel of your foot, an early period, an angry boss, a missed deadline, getting caught in the rain, a hole in your tights, or on the rare occasion being struck by lightning...I could go on, but this triggered way too many flashbacks for me, so I can only imagine what it is doing to you. Did you know at the moment in which you wake and predict that you will have a bad day, it is not, in fact, a given. To be honest, you actually have the power to set the intention of how your day will go, regardless of on which side of the bed you awoke.

I know that some people can relate to a time in your school days where you woke up perfectly fine but decided that you wanted to have a 'bad' day. You may have planned out how you would walk into school, maybe screw up your face, put your hood up, and your sunglasses on. You chose to distance yourself from everyone and sit in the corner, miserable; however, most of the time, it only lasted about five to ten minutes because your friends made you laugh. Trust me, I did this a number of times, and I have to laugh at myself for it because there was no logic or reasoning behind it other than wanting to have a bad day and be in a mood.

If you can choose or plan to have a bad day, you can, indeed, choose to have a good one, or even a great one. This is all dependent on your attitude towards the day.

There are three important steps to having a great day:

One—how you greet the morning sets the initial tone for your day. As soon as you are awake, say out loud, 'GOOD MORNING,' or my personal favourite, 'GRAND RISING.' Remember that you have lived to see another day, a gift that many people do not receive, so let the day know you are grateful, happy, and ready to experience all it has to offer. Greet the day, greet your household, greet your pets, and greet your plants. Let them all know how happy you are to see them live another day.

Two—your morning routine. DO NOT, I REPEAT, DO NOT CHECK YOUR PHONE AS SOON AS YOU WAKE UP! Your emails can wait, social media can wait; it can all wait.

After you have greeted the day, you need to give yourself at least 15 minutes of YOU time. Wake up, stretch or exercise, have a wash, meditate or sit with yourself and reflect. Then, have breakfast, get dressed. Set your intentions for the day by setting yourself three goals or simply write a small paragraph of your expectations and affirmations for the day. *Then* check your phone.

Three—the state of your mind the night before can have a major impact on you the following day. Do not go to bed stressed, upset, angry or anxious. Take 30 minutes before you go to sleep to reflect on the day you just had. Meditate or write a few notes in a journal. Take this time to settle any disagreements you might have had with your partner, friend, family members, or issues at work. If you do not want to discuss the problem, use your journal as a way to release your emotions.

Do what you need to give yourself peace of mind before you go to sleep, otherwise, you will set yourself up for a restless night and a stressful, sleep-deprived day. The importance of sleep is sometimes forgotten, but it plays a vital role when it comes to your physical and mental health. It is important to note that sleep deprivation can cause depression, weight gain, and affect your ability to function, communicate, concentrate, and manage emotions. It can also deteriorate your immune system (Watson and Cherney 2020).

Three steps sound simple enough, but many people struggle to give themselves ten minutes, let alone 20. I understand that life, work, and family can get in the way, but for the sake of your health and wellbeing, you need to dedicate some time in the morning and evening for your reflection, release, and preparation.

Now that you have learnt how to treat the day well once you have implemented these three steps, you will soon see a difference in what you perceive about what goes on around you. Remember that some things are out of your control, but your attitude towards it will dictate how you respond to it. You attract what you put out, so if you put out energies of happiness, love, gratitude, and optimism, the day will reciprocate that energy. You may find yourself receiving opportunities to experience new things, promotions, new friendships, adventures, a newfound love, clearer skies, and you may feel lighter, healthier, happier, and brighter.

It takes 21 days to form a habit and 90 days to make a permanent lifestyle change, so start treating the days well beginning tomorrow, and be open for the day to treat you well in return.

Affirmation: I offer my best self every day and have the power to make each day great.

Lesson 21

'Every key has its own door.'

—Swahili proverb

*W*hether or not you want to believe it, your destination has already been set by the Creator, and the paths you take to get there are your life's journey. You are destined to walk through all the doors marked with your name, and they will open when it is your time.

When you seek your fortune through a door that is not marked for you and make the decision to walk through it regardless, you are, in fact, setting yourself up for failure. I apologise for being blunt, but I have witnessed one too many people lose themselves trying to find success on someone else's path. I have seen people end up stressed, depressed, feeling lost, and even envious of others' successes because they were seeking fulfilment at someone else's door.

I, too, have walked through someone else's door. I saw all the glitter and sparkles and assumed it was for me, too. Instead, I ended up helping them gain all of their success and fortune without considering my own. I spent a year of my life lost and angry, not realising I was angry with myself for not staying true to my path until one day, I found my key, and in turn, I found my door, my path, and the chance to restart my journey.

You see, it is not your door that is hard to find—it is your key!

We are all born with our own unique keys that open all the doors marked for us. The doors may change in size, colour, and location, but the key always remains the same. The only issue is that the place where the key resides can be hard to locate at first. Some people find their keys straight away, and some are guided towards it. For others, it can take a lot longer. There are also those who find their keys, and unfortunately, 'lose' them.

Think of how many times you have lost your house keys. You arrived at your door, reached into your bag or coat pockets, and could not find them anywhere. You started to panic and got frustrated because you were so sure you had them. You searched and searched but still could not seem to locate them until you eventually gave up, but on this particular occasion, you have managed to calm yourself down and decided to do one more check. You reach your hand back into your pocket, and as if by magic, your key is there.

This has happened to me too many times, and I know that some of you can relate to this.

What I am trying to say is that your key is and will always be there because your unique, personalised key is, in fact, your intuition. Your intuition knows what is best for you, and it will guide you to all the doors that belong to you and warn you of those that do not. Your intuition has its own voice. It will call out to you, speak to you, and support you through your life; all you have to do is pay attention and listen. If you choose to not listen to your intuition, the choice to do otherwise can hinder your progress. I know there are many distractions and temptations in this world that cause people to seek what they are looking for externally, rather than internally, but this will inevitably cause you to lose the connection to your intuition. It is also the reason why some people end up losing their keys, and their doors will not open.

All that you need to be successful in this world lies within you. You possess the power—and most importantly, the key—that will guide you to your doors to fulfil your purpose in life bringing happiness, success, love, peace, experience, and more. So, when you feel like you cannot find or hear your key, pause, close your eyes, and take three deep breaths. Listen deeply, and as if by magic, your key will appear and open the doors to all that awaits you.

Affirmation: I listen intently to my intuition and allow it to guide me to all that is mine.

Lesson 22

———•◦•———

'*Affairs of the home should not be discussed in the public square.*'

—Kenyan proverb

I know for a fact that we are all guilty of looking out of the window when we hear our neighbours arguing or fighting in the street. It feels as if the whole world freezes at that moment, and we immediately stop what we are doing, no matter how important it is. We turn down the TV or radio and tell everyone in the house to be silent so we can hear what is going on. Some of us peek our heads out of the window or the door, and there are those who walk boldly outside to see exactly what is going down. At that moment, we all become heavily invested in our neighbors' business, that it becomes our problem or fight, too. You see, this is what happens when you bring the affairs of your home to the public square—or should I say, the streets. It then becomes the street's business, too, and you will have to suffer the repercussions.

Relationships are not always easy. Just like the journey of life, there will be many highs, lows, and bumps on the road. There will be times when you love and adore your partner and times when s/he makes you feel happy, special, and supported, but there will also be times when you loathe them, or they make you angry, upset, or frustrated—I am afraid it is all a part of the package. Besides love, a healthy relationship also requires hard work, dedication, maturity, respect, and reciprocity.

When arguments within your relationship occur, no matter how big or small, it is important to understand that it should be you + your partner versus the problem. In any given circumstance, you must come together as one to tackle the issue(s) at hand, and always focus your attention on the problem rather than the person as a whole. During an argument, if you feel like you are not making progress, you can always take a moment for yourself to think, breathe, re-evaluate, and come back together to solve the problem.

However, when arguments occur, no matter how big or small and you try to approach the problem as you versus your partner versus the problem, this is when issues and breakdowns in communication occur.

This is also why some people take their problems to the public square. In today's society, the public square can be a number of things, such as your friends, family, social media, or literally, the streets.

Many people are quick to message and post their grievances to others before taking a sufficient amount of time and effort to tackle the problem at hand with their partners, but as soon as you bring your arguments to any of these sources, it automatically becomes their business, too. Friends, family and even strangers end up being invested in the affairs of your home, and they may feel the need to give their opinions, which could lead to other arguments. It also places pressure on your close friends and family as they may feel the need to pick sides. I can also be emotionally and mentally draining. The wrong advice can also be given, and they may even push for you to end the relationship, thus creating more problems that you and your partner will have to face outside of your original argument. Even if you resolve your issues, the public forum will continue to discuss your business until the next problem arises.

You and your partner must work together to solve your problems first, before getting others involved. You also need to check your attitude for what you perceive is the problem. This may sound like it is easier said than done, but in truth, it is achievable most of the time. You must also take the time to study and understand your partner, not just their love languages, or what makes them smile but also habits, temperament, triggers, and most importantly, their style of communication. So, when discussions and arguments arise, you both know how to communicate effectively and focus your attention on the issue at hand rather than fighting with each other.

It is important to note that there is nothing wrong with seeking guidance and support from others when you are in need, but you must always remember that everyone does not have your best interests at heart, so be careful to whom you vent. Always seek advice from someone you can both trust, someone who is unbiased, has knowledge, experience, and can help you see both perspectives, such as an elder or a therapist.

The public square is not the place where affairs of your home should be discussed at all, and to those of you dwelling in the public square, always remember to mind the business that pays you!

Affirmation: I choose to build others up rather than tear them down.

Lesson 23

———◆———

*'To neglect one's ancestors will bring
ill-fortune and failure in life.'*

—African proverb

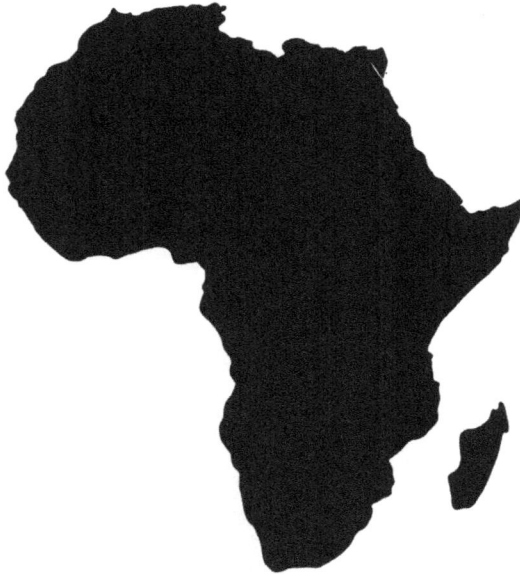

*O*ut of all the lessons I have written, this lesson is the most important: if it were not for my ancestors and the connection I have strived to build and maintain over the years, none of these lessons—or even this book—would have come to fruition. You see, these words you read are not solely mine, but the words of the ancestors who wish to see us better ourselves, learn from the mistakes of the past, heal generational traumas, find our paths, and connect back to our traditions.

Due to the increase of technology and globalisation—or should I say Westernisation—of the planet, many cultures and traditional practices have been altered, lost, forgotten, or even rejected by people across the globe. This is prevalent in the Black community, where some see African cultures, traditions, and practices as outdated, primitive, or even satanic and have turned their backs on their roots. Fortunately, there are still many people who are pushing to keep said culture and traditions alive today, as well as those who no longer wish to be trapped in the Western mindset or society and actively seek to reconnect with their ancestors and African roots. To those of you who read this proverb, saw the word 'ancestors', and felt a sense of fear, evil, or contempt, I ask you to push past these negative, Westernised connotations associated with your ancestors here and now, and allow yourself to read and receive this lesson.

Let us begin.

Our ancestors are, in fact, a part of our genetic makeup, all that we are and encompass. Our DNA, characteristics, likes, dislikes, memories, and experiences are a combination of ourselves and our ancestors through time, space, and history (Spence-Adofo 2020). This is why some people's looks tend to favour their great-grandparents over their parents, why some people have memories from a past life, or the ability to master certain skills and abilities with ease, and why many people have a sense of having been on this earth before.

In a traditional sense, ancestors are people who have passed over to the spiritual realm but are still respected and held to higher esteem by their families or outside communities for what they have done or achieved in their time on earth. Throughout their physical lives, they were positive energies, generous, and influential people who sought to uplift, protect, and support those around them. An ancestor can be a grandparent, elder, parent, sibling, or relative, but it is important to note that ancestors do not necessarily have to be in your bloodline. Rather, you know them for all the work they have done in the community, and you still hold them in high regard. So, even someone in the wider community or known nationally, such as Maya Angelou, Marcus Garvey, or someone further back in history, can still be an ancestor with whom you wish to connect.

As long as their memory is alive in the physical world, they will continue to exist and live in the spiritual realm.

It is important to note that the term 'ancestor' has been generalised to mean anyone who has passed over to the other side in Western society, but this is incorrect. Where issues arise is that not everyone is or can be an ancestor (Conversation with Claud Steven). There are some people on this earth who do not lead positive lifestyles, who are not supportive but are negative, chaotic, or judgemental and do not seek to uplift their families or the wider community. You may have come across these types of people in your life, be they family, friends, partners, colleagues, or even strangers, and at that moment, you knew that you didn't want that type of energy around you. These types of people will not be classed as ancestors in the traditional sense due to their negative energies and ill intentions on earth. Although they are still in the spiritual realm, they should not be called upon at all as this energy will affect you negatively here on earth.

The purpose of our ancestors is to support, guide, and protect us during our journeys in life. When you come across a blockage, if you feel lost, want answers, and need help—whether it has to do with work, relationship, friendships, and finances—you can call on your ancestors to clear the way and give advice and a sense of clarity. There will be times in your life when your intuition is not clear, and your sign from God has yet to arrive, this is where the role of your ancestors comes into play. They are, in essence, an additional support system with whom you can always connect in your time of need. Your ancestors communicate with you in various ways, such as signs, symbols, angel numbers, dreams, visions, and through other people. If you have a stronger connection, you might even be able to hear or physically see them.

If you seek a relationship between you and your ancestors, there are many ways in which you can build your initial connection and welcome them into your life. Altars, pouring libations, and offerings are the best-known ways to communicate with the ancestors.

In brief, an altar is a designated, sacred space and/or table, usually covered in a white cloth or traditional print. On an altar, you will find candles, stones, crystals, water, fresh flowers or a plant, incense, tobacco, and other objects meaningful to you. You can also place pictures of the deceased, specifically, the ancestors with whom you want to connect. The purpose of an altar is to provide you with a sacred space to call and connect with your ancestors. You can also use this space to remember, meditate pray, reflect, and give thanks (Fatunmbi 2020).

Pouring libation is a form of prayer and a way to honour your ancestors. It is a practice that can be found worldwide in both traditional and some Western societies. Libation is usually performed outside, where you pour water or alcohol onto the ground whilst saying a prayer, calling on your ancestors or loved ones, and giving thanks and praise to their lives and memories (Voncujovi 2020).

It is important to note that the relationship between you and your ancestors is reciprocal. It is a continuous cycle of give and take, receiving and giving thanks. This is where the offerings take place. An offering can be a plate of food, fruit, sweets, water, alcohol, flowers, or anything that your ancestors like or have requested. Offerings are used to give thanks, acknowledge your ancestors' support, and show respect for your connection. This is a brief breakdown of the three most used methods to connect to your ancestors; I highly recommend that you do some research prior to creating your connection as there is more to know regarding the 'dos and don'ts', as well as researching ways in which you can connect with your ancestors so you can find out which method is best for you.

When it comes to our ancestors, there is really nothing to fear—they are us, and we are them. We should not neglect those who wish to help and support us, who can guide us when we are lost, warn us of the dangers ahead, and support and uplift us in our times of need. Our ancestors in the spiritual realm are much like the elders on earth who have journeyed through life and gained an abundance of knowledge and wisdom that can be passed down and shared to help navigate our journeys in life. So, when you feel like you have no one to turn to, when your intuition isn't clear, or God has yet to answer you, turn to your ancestors who are always there, ready and willing to help you.

The time has come for us as a people to reconnect to culture, traditions, and our ancestors and allow them to guide us to our freedom.

Affirmation: I choose to connect with my ancestors. I welcome their help and support and will honour their memory every day.

Lesson 24

'*Hold onto a true friend with both hands.*'

—**Nigerian proverb**

*A*t this moment in time, I have three people I consider true friends, real friends, and best friends. I strongly believe these three friendships were put in place by God, as our energies, personalities, and life paths perfectly align, and I have to give thanks to the Creator for blessing me with these three amazing people.

In the past, I have been hurt by people who called themselves 'friends'—a pain I wouldn't wish on anyone. Because of this, I ended up sabotaging many potential friendships as I would not allow people to get close to me and refused to open up my heart due to fear, pain, and anger.

My world changed for the better when these three people walked into my life. I met my first best friend when I was 12, the second at 18, and the third at 22. Over the years, our friendships have blossomed, and we have grown and been through many different experiences together. Most importantly, they have added value to my life and shown me the importance of having true friendships.

Now, if it were not for these three friends, writing this lesson would be extremely hard, but thankfully, I can tell you what a true friend is:

A true friend is someone who supports you, uplifts you, and whom you trust wholeheartedly. A true friend cares about your health and wellbeing as well as her own and makes you laugh and feel good.

A true friend tells you things as they are, even when you do not want to hear it.

A true friend accepts you for who you are, pushes you to do your best, and is there for you during your highest highs and your lowest lows.

A true friend knows you better than you know yourself and uses your words to remind you of the advice you once gave them.

A true friend is someone who compliments your energy, someone you always vibe with.

A true friend is a gift from God. You feel blessed and lucky to have her in your life, and you sometimes treat her better than your own family or vice versa.

Take a moment now to reflect on your current friendships.

How many people do you consider true friends?

What qualities do they possess?

How have they had an impact on your life?

When was the last time you let them know how much you appreciate them?

In life, there will be many people who come and go. As I've said before, some people are here for a reason, season, and a lifetime; this does not only apply to relationships but friendships, too. There will be friends you think are true but end up hurting you, and friends you will outgrow or who will outgrow you. There will also be friendships that simply end for no specific reason. Having at least one true friend in your life can make a whole world of a difference mentally, physically, and spiritually.

I know there are some people who struggle to make friends and those who feel they are out of place within their social groups, or even those who fit into many different groups but do not have a single, true friend. My advice to all of you is the same: take a quiet moment for yourself to write a letter listing all the characteristics and qualities you want in a true friend, every detail and key quality you can think of. Every night before you go to bed, read your letter out loud until you believe this person truly exists and then place the letter somewhere safe. If you can manifest love, money, or a job, you had best believe that you can manifest a true friend into your life, too.

Now, the important thing to note about manifestation is that what you ask for is not always given to you directly. Sometimes opportunities are presented for you to go out to find that for which you are looking. Wherever your intuition guides you during this time, make sure you follow it. Be open to all opportunities, and in time, you will find the true friend you seek.

True friendships are not hard to find once you learn to open your heart, trust others, and believe that you are deserving of a true, loving, and long-lasting friendship. For a friendship to be true, the love must be reciprocated, so make sure you give your friends all the love, respect, and care they give you. Whether you have one true friend, three, or six, hold on to them tightly and never let them go, as true friendships stand the test of time.

Affirmation: I appreciate and cherish my true friends.

Lesson 25

---•◦•---

'If God were not forgiving, heaven would be empty.'

—African proverb

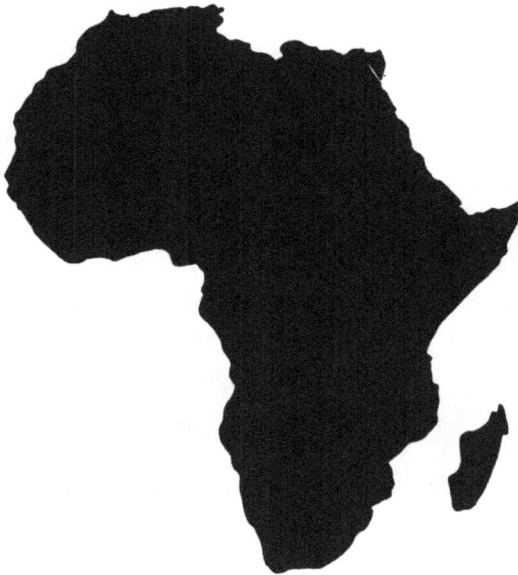

*T*he act of forgiveness is one of the most challenging decisions you will ever have to make in life. I call it an act as it is something that has to be learnt, practised, and put into action. Forgiveness is defined as 'a conscious and voluntary decision to release feelings of resentment or vengeance toward a person(s) who has harmed you, regardless of whether they actually deserve your forgiveness' (Clark 2016). I call it a challenge, as forgiving someone requires mental, emotional, physical, and spiritual strength to decide to release all the pain, trauma, anger, and stress that has built up over time.

In life, there may be situations or people who may hurt you or those you love, people who cross your boundaries, deceive you, or worse, whether it is unintentionally or intentionally. When these negative situations occur, forgiveness is not on most people's minds. Instead, feelings of anger, resentment, fear, hurt, sadness, vengeance, and other emotions take over. Although these feelings are normal, the issue arises when you allow them to harbour and fester in your mind, which, in turn, can cause more pain and suffering, be it mentally, emotionally, physically, or spiritually.

Take a moment now to imagine a dusty sack full of seven bricks. The sack represents the person, thing, or situation you refuse to forgive. The bricks represent all of the thoughts and/or feelings you have been harbouring in your mind for a long period of time. Because you have chosen a path of unforgiveness, your burden is to carry this sack around with you all day, every day, and every night—you are not allowed to put it down at all. I forgot to mention that every brick weighs one stone, and for every person you choose not to forgive, another dusty sack of seven bricks is added to your load.

When you choose a path of unforgiveness, you are, in fact, setting yourself up to carry a very heavy burden.

It is important to understand that forgiveness is for you, the forgiver, and not for the person you need to forgive. To forgive means to understand and accept what has happened. In other words, what is done is done and cannot be undone; therefore, focus your attention on your present self, rather than be held back by your past. To forgive means that you no longer allow any negative emotions or feelings linked to that moment to harbour in your mind—you address them and choose to place them outside of your current reality. To forgive means to take back the power and control in your life, mind, and energy; you are no longer trapped in the moment with those negative feelings, neither are you attached to the person or situation that hurt you. To forgive does not mean forgetting or condoning what has been done to you, but understanding that not everyone apologises, and you have to create peace of mind and freedom for yourself. The only way to truly heal from the wounds inflicted by others is to forgive.

It has taken me sixteen years to forgive someone who hurt me in the past. Sixteen years is a long time to carry that sack around, but I know some people who have been carrying theirs for a lot longer. Choosing not to forgive turned me into an angry, bitter, and depressed person. This, in turn, affected my mental health, and my physical health soon deteriorated, too. No matter how hard I tried to focus on myself, I could not remove this person and the memories from my mind until I learnt how to truly forgive and release her from my life. It was not easy, but in the end, it was worth it.

We live in a world where no one is perfect or without fault, yet God is still willing and able to forgive us all, nevertheless. Forgiveness is like heaven's gates, which are always open. By forgiving others, you allow your heart to remain open to those whose intentions are true.

So, where you can forgive, whether it is forgiving yourself, forgiving others, or asking for forgiveness, set yourself free and be at peace, always.

Affirmation: Today, I choose forgiveness over anger.
I forgive myself for the mistakes I have made. I forgive others who have hurt me and release all negative attachments and feelings.
Today, I choose my peace of mind.

Lesson 26

---•◦•---

'Lack of knowledge is darker than the night.'

—African proverb

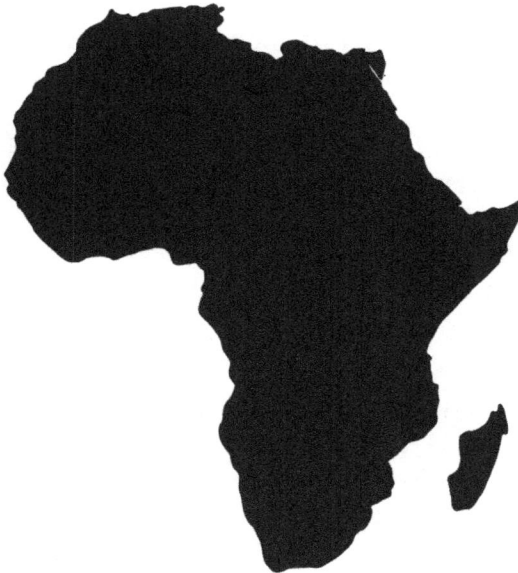

*T*he night is when we are most vulnerable, and during the darkest of nights, anything can happen.

In the darkest of nights, your mind starts to play tricks on you, you imagine strange figures, hear weird noises, and a sense of fear overwhelms you. The dark makes you blind to all that surrounds you, and on the darkest of nights, you will not know which way is forward, what dangers lie ahead, or who is lurking in the shadows. On the darkest of nights, anyone can take you and make you believe they are guiding you to the light or somewhere safe.

The truth is that we live in a society run by those who dwell in the dark. They are the shadows and strange figures that play tricks on us. They act as if they are offering help and support, but in truth, they guide us further into the darkness that is ignorance, and they will do anything in their power to keep us there. Through their system of oppression or institutions, money, politics, false leaders and/or prophets, fake news, TV, social media, and celebrities, they are able to manipulate and entice people to stay in the darkness.

It is up to us to use the power of knowledge to find our way out of the dark!

Ignorance is 'making the conscious decision to not learn, and improve your understanding on a topic, or consider another source of information as valid' (Mirchevski 2020).

To be ignorant in today's society is not at all blissful but extremely harmful, not only to yourself but others and society as a whole. You can be led down the wrong path by someone who is just as ignorant as you or someone who uses their knowledge to manipulate you.

There are people who speak on topics about which they have minimal knowledge, and they spread information they have not first researched or clarified for themselves, as well as those who have opinions on topics and who speak without authority. You may have come across someone like this in your life before, whether it was during a family discussion, someone online, or a political figure, or you may have been the one who has spoken about a topic without knowledge, as we have all been guilty of this. Everyone has something to say, and you may think that what you know is right and enough, but it is important to understand that whether you are in a position of power or an ordinary person, words still have power, and they can influence the actions of others.

In a world full of access to information, education, and learning, whether it is through the Internet, books, journals, courses, teachers, or elders, ignorance is, indeed, a choice in today's society. In truth, ignorance has become somewhat of a culture in itself, as many people are collectively choosing to remain in the dark, ignorant of the facts available to them. To be ignorant is to be fearful of change or the unknown. It is to be wrong and exposed to not knowing everything, which can cause some people to avoid the truth of the knowledge to protect their reality and all they know to be true.

When you gain more knowledge, you, in turn, gain a new perspective on life.

Your old habits fade, your mind expands, your social circle may change, and you may question your reality or become more aware of yourself and those around you.

The road to gaining knowledge is not easy; it requires a lot of hard work and determination to relinquish control and allow your mind to be open to receiving new information. It also requires you to sift through all the fake information and opinions, as well as look through multiple sources to ensure what you have learnt is, indeed, fact. The only true way out of the darkness of ignorance is by gaining more knowledge and educating yourself.

Knowledge is the path that will guide you out of the darkness and into the light.

Knowledge is the power that will protect you on this journey, guide you to where it is safe, and keep the tricksters at bay.

It is time for us as a collective to start a new culture of examining the knowledge that is available to us, rather than blindly accepting knowledge given to us by those who want us to stay in the dark.

So, if you are ready to step out of the darkness, pick a topic and start researching.

Affirmation: I am open to receive and examine new information and knowledge. I am learning and growing into a more informed person every day.

Lesson 27

—•◦•—

'The world has not made a promise to anybody.'

—Moroccan proverb

*O*ur time as humans on this earth is temporary; it always has been and always will be. If the world were to end tomorrow, would you be content with all you achieved in your life so far?

I want to make a key distinction between what we view as the Earth and the world.

The Earth is a living planet that all creatures call home. It is filled with plants, animals, mammals, water, and the land that sustains us. The world, however, encompasses the manmade structures and societies created by us to maintain and live as a species on this planet. This includes our structures, infrastructures, cultures, institutions, laws, values, and norms.

The world is a complex place where we all have to find our way and establish our purpose amongst others.

Finding your purpose in this world is not easy, but it is not hard either. It all depends on how willing you are to listen to your inner-self and let it guide you. There are those who are born knowing their purpose in life, and those who forget and then find their way back years later. There are also those who do not believe they have a divine purpose, or they let the opinions of others stop them from fulfilling their purpose.

Take a moment now to reflect on your current life.

What do you truly want to achieve in your life?

Are you aware of your purpose?

Do you even believe that you have a purpose on this earth?

In life, there are many distractions, negative energies, situations, and people who will block your path and hinder your progress. Even the system in which we live today was created for the purpose of suppressing and controlling people's minds and lifestyles, but you must learn to push past and overcome all challenges if you want to live a fulfilling life. Always remember that it is your life, your path, your story, and you hold the key to your success. When you actively choose to fulfil your purpose, many paths will be paved, doors will open, and the right people will flow into your life to help you reach your goals.

It took me a number of years to find my purpose in this world. I spent years questioning my existence and abilities. I lacked confidence in myself and hated God for putting me on this planet without a purpose, but the truth is that I was born knowing my purpose. I knew exactly what I was here to do from a very young age, but I simply did not believe that I could achieve it, so rather than waste my time trying and failing, I decided to let the distractions of the world take over. When I made the active decision to start loving myself, believe in my skills and abilities, and connect back to God, my ancestors, and my intuition, everything in my life fell into place, and my purpose made its way to me. Since then, I have continued to align my life with my purpose, and I will never stray from it again.

Understand that no single person is greater than another, and everyone's purpose in this world is equally important. We are all destined for greatness and to lead fulfilling lives. Greatness is not something you will find on the outside, nor will it be awarded to you by others, although the world will lead you to believe it is. Greatness is an energy that comes from within. It should not be measured or compared. When you take the time to understand and accept who you are as well as learn to love and improve yourself, you are, in turn, becoming your greatest self. As long as you are living, it is never too late—you still have time to fulfil all you want to achieve in life.

The world owes us nothing. We are simply spiritual beings having a physical experience for a set amount of time. Now, I cannot tell you what your purpose is—that is something you must figure out on your own—but know that God has already provided you with the skills, ability, and talent to help you align with your purpose on this earth.

So, no matter what you choose to do with your time on this physical plane, be aware that there are no second chances or redos, make the best out of what the world has to offer.

Affirmation: Every day I honour my purpose by being my greatest self.

Lesson 28

———◦•◦———

'Make a bed for the children of other people in the place where your own children sleep.'

—Morrocan proverb

*B*eing a parent is not easy, it is one of the most physically and mentally demanding roles you could ever have. Although I am not a parent myself—and in truth, I am dreading the day—I am still someone's child, and I know how difficult it can be to raise children whilst trying to balance everything else. Being a parent means sacrificing your time, energy, money, life, and for mothers, their bodies, to cater to all the needs of your children. Raising children in today's society is particularly difficult, as most parents juggle work, life, relationships, and health, whilst trying to bring up well-rounded, healthy, educated, respectful, and loved children. Unfortunately, not everyone has the luxury of being able to afford childcare or have close friends and family who are willing and able to help.

This is why we must look back to our African culture and traditions, where the village comes together as one collective to raise the children. Within the village, parents, grandparents, uncles, aunties, elders, friends, and neighbours share all of the duties and responsibilities, using the time to teach and impart their own wisdom, experiences, and knowledge to the children. Sharing this enormous responsibility creates a safe space where parents can share their experiences and the weight of parenting, learn from the mistakes of others, and support one another. This also allows parents to find balance within their personal lives and dedicate enough time to their work, health, relationships, and family as a whole. A good village creates a safe space where children can learn from those around them, experience different parenting styles, socialise with other children and families, build healthy connections, and be supported and guided through every stage of their childhood, as well as being loved and protected by the village as a whole, thus creating a healthier, stable environment in which to grow.

However, this is not always the case in modern Western society and culture, as it is less about the village dynamic and about the nuclear family. This mindset alone causes people to focus solely on the needs of their households, and have the tendency to portray themselves as strong, self-reliant, in control, and independent. This individualistic mindset has, in turn, broken down many communities and the village framework as we no longer support, uplift, respect, or trust one another as a collective. As a parent, this mindset causes more harm than good, as you are more likely to be isolated from others, stressed, depressed, and pressured to figure things out on your own. You may even be less likely to reach out to people in your times of need, whether it is due to fear, shame, pride, or seeing offers of help as people overstepping.

As a child, you need someone who is there for you physically, emotionally, and socially to provide all of your essential needs, but parents who do not have enough time and energy for their children or who do not have a village on which to rely simply cannot provide this. When a child's needs are not being met, it can result in many adverse effects, such as low self-esteem, a lack of social skills, anxiety, depression, and behavioural problems (Healthline 2019). Some children become self-reliant adults before their time, and they may seek what they have been missing from their parents elsewhere— be it is attention, love, gratification, empathy, or support—and it is why some children turn to drugs, gangs, the Internet or other people they view as role models.

Being a parent is not easy. There is not a guidebook on how to raise children successfully, but there are those around you who have the knowledge and experience to help you on your journey of parenthood. The time has truly come for us to rebuild our villages for the sake of both the children and the parents. We must come together as a collective to create a safe space and environment in which children can grow and learn.

Let us fill our villages with those who will support, uplift, nurture, love, protect, respect, and teach not only the children but parents, too, who, in turn, will do the same for the next generations.

Affirmation: I offer my help and support to all those in need. I accept all offers of help and support when I am in need.

Lesson 29

———◆••◆———

*'When the white man is about to leave
the garden, he wrecks it.'*

—Yoruba proverb

*A*llow me to tell you a story...

Once upon a time, the original people of this earth lived in harmony with nature. They respected, cared for, and nurtured the land around them. They knew that the earth provided more than enough sustenance for them to live off, from freshwater, food, herbs, fire, and materials with which to make clothes, tools, and shelters. The original people were, in fact, the caretakers of this earth. They knew to take only what was necessary and reciprocate for all the earth had provided them. The relationship between man and earth was one of love, respect, and honour, like a bond between a child and their mother, and this connection was more than physical; it was spiritual, too. As time passed, the original people travelled across the earth to explore new lands. They went from continent to continent, sharing their knowledge and understanding. Some settled in these new places while others simply passed through and some got lost along the way.

For centuries, man was in balance with nature until one day, the descendants of the lost ones left their garden and went in search of a new one.

You see, the lost ones had been living in the icy cold barren lands, where the warmth of the earth ceased to exist. Although they were the descendants of the original people, this memory and connection had long been forgotten, as the harshness of the cold had infected their brains and turned them into bitter, angry, distrustful, and aggressive people.

As the years went on, this bitterness turned into violence and warfare. The lost ones spent most of their time at war with each other, and their garden was constantly watered with the blood of others. The respect and love for the earth ceased to exist, and they continued to destroy and mistreat it, along with the living creatures and their fellow people.

As time passed, the lost ones grew tired of their garden. There was not enough space or any fresh food or water as it all had been tainted with blood, faeces, and rodents. So, the lost ones went in search of something better.

The lost ones soon found the garden they were looking for. In fact, they found many better gardens, and at that moment, decided they could not just have one, and they must have them all. A fit of rage and jealousy took over the lost ones who were mad that earth had not provided them with anything, whilst all the other people had been living in the abundant warmth.

Then, a moment of fear came over them, the fear of going back to living a life of lack and scarcity, the fear of the people who were stronger and had more knowledge than them, the fear that they would not allow them to live with them. Little did they know, the descendants of the original people respected all those the earth had birthed, and they wished to educate and share the wisdom that had been passed down through the generations with them. Harm would never come to them so long as they respected them and the earth.

The lost one's distrustful nature took over their minds, and they thought that the only way for them to have the garden was to remove the people who were currently living there. What followed can only be described as an act of worldwide destruction, chaos, and mass terrorism, not only of the people but of the earth, too. The lost ones went from continent to continent, soiling the earth with the blood of its people, infecting the land with pain, fear, suffering, and the bodies of those who had once loved and cared for the earth.

Even though the lost ones took over all the gardens they wanted, they continued to mistreat them, just like an abuser who constantly mistreats their victim for no other reason than to keep control and maintain power and dominance. The lost ones knew that power over the earth meant power over the people.

What were once abundant gardens and lands were soon barren and wrecked. As the years passed, most of the original people's descendants fell under the spell of the lost ones, and they turned their backs on the earth and left it vulnerable for the taking. The years of pain and suffering they endured caused them to forget their connection and responsibility to the earth.

The earth knew a change would soon come, as life is about cycles, and everything has an end and a new beginning. Where there is an imbalance, a fight to restore balance is sure to follow.

So, the earth continued to fight back and send signs to warn the people, even though they continued to suck her dry. This struck fear into the lost ones, the same fear their predecessors felt when they saw the original people, and they knew their time in the warmth of the sun would soon be over.

Either the earth was truly dying, or it was time for the descendants of the original people to take their rightful place as caretakers of the earth to restore balance. So, to spite the earth, the lost ones continued to drain her, every mineral, nutrient, and vitamin. They burnt the land, beat it, cut it down, polluted the air, and poisoned the water. Then, they soiled the earth with more blood and continued to manipulate the rest of humanity to do the same to ensure that no one would reap the rewards of the earth's abundant love after them.

The end.

Now, this is just a story. It is neither fact nor fiction, but it is a story I was called to share, regardless. You must know that a change is coming. Although I cannot tell you what that change is, I can tell you that the time has come for us to connect back to the earth. The time has come to heal and restore the natural balance of the world and right the wrongs of those who came before us. Regardless of our races or ethnicities, we all have the duty and responsibility to heal the earth before it is too late.

Affirmation: I will care, respect, and love the Earth.
I will only take what I need and reciprocate all that
the Earth has provided.

Lesson 30

'*Everything has an end.*'

—**Tanzanian proverb**

*W*hen a stage in our lives comes to an end, it is the universe creating a space for a new beginning to enter. So, whether it is a relationship, a time at a specific place, a job, a friendship, or life itself, do not fear, worry, or be upset. Understand that a new beginning or stage of being is on its way. Even when we pass over and our physical time on this earth ends, our spirits return to the spiritual realm, where we begin a new chapter of existence.

So, where there is an end, there will always be a new beginning.

We have reached the last lesson of this guidebook, and your new beginning has been patiently waiting since you read the first lesson. The time has come to take what you have learnt from each proverb and apply it to your everyday life. Always remember that you can refer back to this book at any moment of your life as this was not created to be read just once or page by page, but to be opened at any time, place, and page to meet the needs of the particular moment or specific guidance you seek.

As I said at the beginning of this book, these proverbs will always be relevant.

Whether you are reading them in 2021 or in the distant future, they transcend through space and time. These lessons are just as relevant as they were in the past when they were spoken in their traditional setting, as they are today. So, by the time you pass this book on to the next generation, it should be well-worn, showing how much you have used and returned to the lessons during your life's journey, truly expressing the wisdom within the words, and the guidance they provide.

Remember that you possess all you need to be successful and lead a fulfilling life. Should you forget, this book will always be here to remind you.

Affirmation: I am open to the opportunity and change this new beginning brings.

A Mantra

A mantra that was spoken throughout my childhood,
and something I wish to share with you:
'We have faith in ourselves and our people,
We have the power to make our dreams reality,
To overcome any obstacles we may meet,
We will our lives in divine truth, justice, and harmony,
To be the best that we can be,
So we can stand up proud and say,
Look at us, we are great!'

—A.S.K. (Aimhotep School of Knowledge)

About the Author

Kesi Steven is a British-born Caribbean woman, raised in a home where she was taught that she can be, and achieve anything her heart desires. This freedom has allowed her to explore, create, and become the free thinking and speaking woman she is today. Kesi is passionate about many things from creative writing, art and design, filmmaking, Afrocentrism, spiritualism, storytelling, and has a natural gift for bringing what she desires into reality.

Kesi created her first written piece in 2019 for Black History Month called 'Mirror Mirror on the Wall -Who's The Black Girl Standing Tall?'. A message for not only herself but the Black community as a whole, to learn and understand the power of loving yourself for who you are and the importance of learning your true history.

This written piece caused an awakening and unlocked Kesi's true passion for writing; specifically storytelling, words of wisdom, advice and healing.

Leading her to create her first book 'A Guide to Life', which incorporates the same message from her previous works of self-love, healing, the power of being black, knowing our history, and learning from those that came before us.

Bibliography

————————•◦•————————

Academy, C., Course, F., Mvula, K., Hub, C., B, G. and prophet, N., 2020. *The Secret Of Change (Don't Listen To Socrates) | Enclaria: Influence Change At Work.* [online] Enclaria.com. Available at: <https://www.enclaria.com/2018/10/25/the-secret-of-change-dont-listen-to-socrates/>[Accessed 8 April 2020].

Andersen, D., 2017. *How Many Bridges Are There In The World? - Quora.* [online] Quora.com. Available at: <https://www.quora.com/How-many-bridges-are-there-in-the-world> [Accessed 30 March 2020].

BBC News. 2020. *Africa's Proverb Of The Day.* [online] Available at: <https://www.bbc.co.uk/news/world-africa-18930368> [Accessed 2 February 2020].

Center for Creative Leadership. 2020. *What Are The Characteristics Of A Good Leader? | CCL.* [online] Available at: <https://www.ccl.org/blog/characteristics-good-leader/> [Accessed 26 July 2020].

Clark, P., 2016. *The Power Of Forgiveness.* [online] Medium. Available at: <https://medium.com/thrive-global/the-power-of-forgiveness.> [Accessed 22 September 2020].

de Ley, G., 2019. *The Book Of African Proverbs*. New York: Hatherleigh Press.

Duff, K., 2016. *5 Things Every Procrastinator Says To Justify Procrastinating*. [online] The Odyssey Online. Available at: <https://www.theodysseyonline.com/5-things-procrastinator-justify-procrastinating> [Accessed 15 July 2020].

Fatunmbi, A., n.d. *Ancestor Reverence: Building An Ancestor Shrine*. [online] Africaspeaks.com. Available at: <http://www.africaspeaks.com/reasoning/index.php?topic=2775.0;wap2> [Accessed 11 August 2020].

Gammon, K., 2020. *What's The World's Longest Bridge?*. [online] livescience.com. Available at: <https://www.livescience.com/34448-worlds-longest-bridge.html.> [Accessed 18 March 2020].

Geography.name. 2020. *Africa: Age And Aging*. [online] Available at: <https://geography.name/age-and-aging/> [Accessed 11 July 2020].

GoodTherapy.org Therapy Blog. 2020. *Love - Goodtherapy.Org Therapy Blog*. [online] Available at: <https://www.goodtherapy.org/blog/psychpedia/love/> [Accessed 20 July 2020].

Healthline. 2019. *Childhood Emotional Neglect: What It Is, And How It Can Affect You*. [online] Available at: <https://www.healthline.com/health/mental-health/childhood-emotional-neglect#symptoms-in-children> [Accessed 26 September 2020].

Hocken, V., 2020. *The Full Moon*. [online] Timeanddate.com. Available at: <https://www.timeanddate.com/astronomy/moon/full-moon.html> [Accessed 17 April 2020].

Hocken, V., Bikos, K. and Jones, G., 2021. *What Causes Ocean Tides?*. [online] Timeanddate.com. Available at: <https://www.timeanddate.com/astronomy/moon/tides.html> [Accessed 11 May 2020].

Johnson, L., 2020. *10 Oldest Bridges In The World – Oldest.Org*. [online] Oldest.org. Available at: <https://www.oldest.org/structures/bridges/> [Accessed 6 July 2020].

Jones, C., 2019. *The Symbolism Of Walls*. [online] Medium. Available at: <https://medium.com/thinksheet/the-symbolism-of-walls-bbb50f644bd8> [Accessed 11 June 2020].

Kornei, K., 2017. *How Many Tree Species Are There? More Than You Can Shake A Stick At, New Database Reveals*. [online] Science | AAAS. Available at: <https://www.sciencemag.org/news/2017/04/how-many-tree-species-are-there-more-you-can-shake-stick-new-database-reveals> [Accessed 30 August 2020].

Matador Network. 2020. *50 African Proverbs To Get You Thinking*. [online] Available at: <https://matadornetwork.com/bnt/50-african-proverbs-to-get-you-thinking/> [Accessed 2 September 2020].

Mirchevski, B., 2020. *In The Age Of Information, Ignorance Is A Choice*. [online] Medium. Available at: <https://medium.com/the-logician/in-the-age-of-information-ignorance-is-a-choice-2dc8f4efe764> [Accessed 20 September 2020].

OriginsInfo. 2017. *What's In A Name? Name Traditions Of Africa - Originsinfo*. [online] Available at: <https://www.originsinfo.com.au/whats-in-a-name-name-traditions-of-africa/> [Accessed 11 July 2020].

"Peace of Mind." Dictionary.com. 2020. [online] Available at: <https://www.dictionary.com/e/slang/peace-of-mind/> [Accessed 30 February 2020].

Scientific American. 2015. *How Many Trees Are There In The World?*. [online] Available at: <https://www.scientificamerican.com/article/how-many-trees-are-there-in-the-world-video/> [Accessed 30 August 2020].

Sogoba, M., 2019. *The Power Of A Name | Cultures Of West Africa*. [online] Cultures of West Africa. Available at: <https://www.culturesofwestafrica.com/power-of-names/> [Accessed 11 July 2020].

Spence-Adofo, V., 2020. *Ancestral Voices | Communicating With Your Ancestors*. [online] Ancestralvoices.co.uk. Available at: <https://ancestralvoices.co.uk/communicating-with-your-ancestors/> [Accessed 15 September 2020].

Voncujovi, S., 2020. *5 Steps To Offer Libation To Your Ancestors*. [online] Medium. Available at: <https://voncujovi-s.medium.com/5-steps-to-offer-libation-to-your-ancestors-2a888348ae5a> [Accessed 29 December 2020].

Watson, S. and Cherney, K., 2020. *11 Effects Of Sleep Deprivation On Your Body*. [online] Healthline. Available at: <https://www.healthline.com/health/sleep-deprivation/effects-on-body> [Accessed 4 August 2020].

Wensjoe, J., 2020. *The Art Of Ballet*. [online] Theatreinparis.com. Available at: <https://www.theatreinparis.com/blog/the-art-of-ballet> [Accessed 30 September 2020].

Worldometers.info. 2020. *World Population Clock: 7.8 Billion People (2020) - Worldometer*. [online] Available at: <https://www.worldometers.info/world-population/> [Accessed 15 June 2020].

Wow4u.com. 2020. *61 African Proverbs - Inspirational Words Of Wisdom*. [online] Available at: <https://www.wow4u.com/african-proverbs/> [Accessed 2 March 2020].

Conscious Dreams
PUBLISHING

Be the author of your own destiny

Find out about our authors, events, services and how you can get your book journey started.

Conscious Dreams Publishing

@DreamsConscious

@consciousdreamspublishing

Daniella Blechner

www.consciousdreamspublishing.com

info@consciousdreamspublishing.com

Let's connect

www.ingramcontent.com/pod-product-compliance
Lightning Source LLC
Chambersburg PA
CBHW030254030426
42336CB00009B/381